WORLD SPECTATORS

Cultural Memory
in
the
Present

Mieke Bal and Hent de Vries, Editors

WORLD
SPECTATORS

Kaja Silverman

STANFORD

UNIVERSITY

PRESS

STANFORD,

CALIFORNIA

Stanford University Press
Stanford, California

Diagram in Chapter 4 from Sigmund Freud, *Interpretation
of Dreams* (S. E. 5:541), © 1953 A. W. Freud et al., by
arrangement with Mark Paterson & Associates.

Chapter 6 epigraph from "Correspondences," in *The Flowers
of Evil*, by Charles Baudelaire, translated by James McGowan
(1993), reprinted by permission of Oxford University Press.

Printed in the United States of America

Library of Congress Cataloging-in-Publication Data

Silverman, Kaja.
    World spectators / Kaja Silverman.
        p.   cm. — (Cultural memory in the present)
    Includes bibliographical references (p.   ) and index.
      ISBN 0-8047-3831-9 (alk. paper) — ISBN 0-8047-3832-7
(paper : alk. paper)
      1. Phenomenalism.   2. Appearance (Philosophy)
3. Psychoanalysis and philosophy.   4. Vision.   I. Title.
II. Series.
BD352 .S55   2000
190—dc21   00-041052

Original printing 2000

Last figure below indicates year of this printing:
09   08   07   06   05   04   03   02   01   00

For Leo Bersani,
my self in difference.

ACKNOWLEDGMENTS

I could not have written *World Spectators* without the help of many German and American friends. Late-night conversations with Fred Dolan about Hannah Arendt inspired me to read first her, and then Heidegger. They thus mark a major turning point in my life. Certain key parts of my argument came into sharp focus for me for the first time during a series of important exchanges with Eric Santner. I was intellectually sustained throughout the writing of this book by my many meetings and telephone conversations with Leo Bersani. Ulla Ziemann's photographs and our discussions about them provided me with a constant, radiant example of what I was writing about. And my relationship with Harun Farocki was the precondition for thinking every one of the thoughts upon which *World Spectators* is based.

I am also enormously indebted to a number of my former and present graduate students, who participated in the seminars in which I worked through many parts of this book. Six of them— Rob Miotke, Homay King, Greg Forter, Maria St. John, Eve Meltzer, and Joel Nickels—also read and responded to *World Spectators* with a diligence, generosity and acumen which I can only dream of emulating. Rob Miotke, Greg Forter, and Eve Meltzer also served as my research assistants at different moments in the writing of this book and kept up the extraordinarily high standard previously established by Amy Zilliax.

A group of preeminent classicists—Page du Bois, Shadi Bartsch, Ramona Naddof, David Cohen, Mark Griffith, and Jill Spicer—

read Chapter 1 of this volume, and made suggestions for revisions and further readings. I want to thank them for their exceptional courtesy, and to voice the hope that they will not have cause to regret being mentioned here. Judith Butler and Mieke Bal read an earlier draft of this book, and gave me invaluable assistance in improving it. Finally, I am indebted to Jörg Becker for his indispensable last-minute research assistance, and to Tony Newcomb for helping me to secure the time I needed to write this book.

K.S.

Berlin, July 1999

CONTENTS

WORLD SPECTATORS

1

SEEING FOR THE SAKE OF SEEING

As has oft been noted, Western philosophy began with the turn away from the world of the senses to a suprasensual domain.[1] Plato's Socrates,[2] who made this event an exemplum for all right-thinking men, also immortalized it in the parable of the cave.[3] In this most famous of all philosophical allegories, a prisoner who has been imprisoned in a dark cave since childhood, and who spends his time looking at shadows cast on the wall in front of him by a complicated projection system, is released from his chains and delivered into the sunlight outside. The cave stands for our mundane world, and the region outside for that higher reality from which everything—including our world—ostensibly derives.

In his interpretation of the parable, Socrates maintains that this turn away from the world is spiritual in nature; it is the soul, he tells Glaucon, which moves from the "realm of becoming to the realm of what is" (521d). Since the allegory itself contains so many references to the physical rigors of the prisoner's ascent—the path leading out of the cave is "rough" and "steep" (515e), for instance, and the light outside irritatingly bright (515e–516a)—it often seems to suggest a diametrically opposed notion of what it means to approach the suprasensory domain. But regardless of whether Socrates emphasizes the spiritual or physical nature of this journey, it is always to the look that he returns. I will attempt to show that this is because the turn away from the world is definitionally a visual event. It entails the reorientation—or, more precisely, the *disorientation*—of vision. To abandon the domain of phenomenal forms is, quite simply, to lose one's sight.

This is not, of course, how Socrates himself accounts for the journey toward the Good. For him, the turn away from the world is scopically liberating. The man who looks at shadows on the cave wall is in prison, visually speaking. He is enslaved by appearance. He attributes reality to what are in fact representations of representations—accepts as true what only *seems* (515b–c). This man also attributes reality to what emerges from darkness and disappears once again in it—to what "wander[s] around between coming to be and decaying" (485b).[4] True vision is what we achieve only when all representational mediation has been removed; only when we are face to face with the self-present, the self-same, that which forever Is.[5]

What I have just summarized is, of course, that long dream of metaphysics from which Nietzsche roused us.[6] However, the parable of the cave sustains other dreams than that of Socrates. It provides one of the supports for Heidegger's account of a premetaphysical truth, a truth inhering less in correctness of representation than in the unhiding of the hidden.[7] It also serves as one of the textual bases for Arendt's postmetaphysical inversion of the spiritual over the sensual.[8] And in this chapter, the parable of the cave will supply the coordinates for yet another antiplatonic account of our relation to the phenomenal domain. I will be using it to dream in an anticipatory way about world spectatorship:[9] about a kind of looking which takes place *in* the world, and *for* the world—a kind of looking which not only stubbornly adheres to phenomenal forms, but also augments and enriches them. Through the parable of the cave and the other texts that I will group around it, I will also be arguing that to be a world spectator is not to content oneself with seeming to the exclusion of Being, but rather to commit oneself to remaining within the only domain where Being can emerge, the domain of appearance.

I mentioned Heidegger's and Arendt's readings of Plato's most famous allegory above because both also rigorously challenge the opposition of Being and appearance which is at the heart of Socrates' account of vision. For Heidegger, the parable of the cave helps us to understand that appearance is not an inaccurate replica of Being, but rather is its mode of "stepping forth." It is the extrusion through which Being "presents" itself (164). For Arendt, the shadow-watching in which Socrates' prisoners engage is a privileged instantiation of what she calls the "it-appears-to-me."[10] The it-appears-to-me, in turn, is one of the concepts by means of which Arendt not only celebrates the domain of appearance over that of an ever present and unchanging truth, but also equates it with Being itself.[11]

But although these two philosophers share my conviction that appearance is the locus within which Being unfolds, rather than its binary opposite, they define it very differently than I will be defining it here. Appearance is generally a metaphor for Heidegger and Arendt of a primarily linguistic disclosure. In "Letter on Humanism"[12] and a number of subsequent texts,[13] Heidegger identifies language as the privileged domain for the unconcealment of Being. Although for the Arendt of *The Human Condition* and *On Revolution* it is primarily within the arena of political action that appearance occurs, here again language—along with action—plays the central role.[14] My emphasis will instead be insistently visual. I will be defining "appearance" in the strictest sense of that word, as a coming forward into view or becoming visible. At the same time, this apparent semantic narrowing down will actually result in an opening up, since visibility will be shown to depend upon a confluence of the phenomenal, the psychic, the specular, and the social.

METAPHORS OF VISION

Heidegger claims in *An Introduction to Metaphysics* that the Greeks "had no word for 'space,'"[15] at least not as we conceptualize it today. It might seem that this is the reason why it is so difficult for us to orient ourselves spatially when reading the parable of the cave. The metaphors through which Socrates allegorizes the journey toward the Good in book 7 of the *Republic* keep changing, until we no longer know where we are.

The first metaphor that Socrates uses to describe how we come to the Good is "turning around." He deploys the verb *to turn* both when recounting his strange story and when explaining what it means. The prisoner who is released from his bondage in front of the shadows on the cave wall must first turn around to see the puppets responsible for those shadows (515c, d). The philosopher's journey away from the inessential toward the essential involves a similar conversion. The seeker after truth must turn his "whole soul" until he is "able to study that which is and the brightest thing that is, namely, the one we call the good" (518c, d).

After the prisoner turns around, he must ascend. Although this ascent begins with his physical journey out of the cave, Socrates describes it primarily in visual terms. First the prisoner "looks" at the fire at the back of the cave (515c). Later, out in the open, he "sees" the "shadows" and then the "images of men and other things in water." Eventually, the liberated man apprehends "the things themselves" (516a). From here he goes on "to [look] at the light of the stars and the moon," and finally "the sun and the light of the sun" (516a–b).

When Socrates glosses this part of the allegory, he introduces a new metaphor. In our original human condition, he tells us, we are souls burdened by the leaden weights of "becoming," anchored to the earth (519a–b). Only if these weights are removed can we gain access to "true things" (519b). In order to make sense of the last part of this new metaphor, which works on a vertical rather than a horizontal axis, we must imagine some kind of action on the part of the soul—a flying or soaring upward toward the Good. However, Socrates does not complete the metaphor in this way. Instead, he has recourse once again to the metaphor of vision. And, although he initially combines the metaphor of seeing with the metaphor of the leaden weights, suggesting that the weights pull vision "downwards" (519b), he abandons this vertical metaphor a moment later. The look which is released from the leaden weights does not lose its gravity. Rather, its capacity to apprehend the Good is "sharp[ened]" (519b).

As should be clear by now, there is only one metaphor to which Socrates remains constant throughout this part of the *Republic*, and that is the metaphor of sight. No matter how much he mixes or varies his tropes, he always returns to the look. Vision achieves its privileged status as a signifier for the soul, however, only by being undone as such—only by being thoroughly negated as a scopic activity. This is the real reason why the spatial coordinates of the cave are so confusing. If we have a difficult time keeping our balance while reading the parable of the cave, it is not because of the semantic limitations of classical Greek, but rather because of the deformation to which Socrates subjects the look, to whose coordinates our sense of space is keyed.[16]

UNDOING THE LOOK

Although the turning around of the prisoner from the visible to the invisible begins with the unfastening of his shackles, the notion of a liberation is strangely difficult to map onto what follows. The prisoner is no sooner unfettered than he is forced to stand up, turn his head, and walk and look toward the light, an obligation which "pain[s]" and "dazzle[s]" him (515c). He is subsequently "dragged . . . away" from the cave "by force, up the rough, steep path," and required to step into the sunlight (515e). Again Socrates notes that the prisoner is "pained" and "irritated" by this treatment (515e). He also tells us three different times that the latter's emancipation is effected under compulsion (515c–e). The leaden weights metaphor which Socrates deploys in his interpretation of the allegory also works at cross-purposes with the notion of freedom. In order to be released from the weights of becoming, the future philosopher must be "hammered at from childhood" (519a).

As Socrates himself openly acknowledges at one point in his interpretation of the cave allegory, it is primarily upon the organ of vision that this violence is enacted. Not surprisingly, then, when the prisoner returns to the cave after his sojourn outside he has lost his capacity to participate in the shadow game he played before. The other prisoners complain that his eyesight has been "ruined" by his journey out of the cave (517a). As if to muffle the worrisome reverberations of this word, Socrates tells Glaucon that there are two kinds of blindness—the kind which afflicts the prisoner when he first turns away from the shadows on the cave wall to the greater brightness behind him, and the kind from which he suffers when he returns to the cave (518a, b). Whereas the former is the result of the prisoner not yet having learned how to see, the latter might be said to be the result of a hyperacuity of vision. However, later in book 7 we learn that those who would apprehend the Good must quite simply "relinquish [their] eyes" (537d).[17]

Socrates makes it even more evident in book 6 of the *Republic* that the agency to which his philosophical project is so inimical is visual. He compares the liberated soul there to an eye which not merely attaches itself raptly to the sun, but also derives its power to see from that solar body, "like an influx from an overflowing treasure" (508a, b). Human vision is thus elevated to the status of a metaphor for metaphysical contemplation only by being reduced to a pure receptivity. Socrates also suggests in book 6 of the *Republic* that, in addition to providing the earthly analogue for spiritual enlightenment, this subordination of the look represents a necessary stage in the journey toward such enlightenment. Whereas the trope of the cave is the primary one in book 7, that of the line predominates in book 6 (509d–511e). And, whereas the passage in which Socrates interprets the parable of the cave stresses the discontinuity between earthly terms and their heavenly counterparts, the passage in which he explains the line makes what happens in earthly experience the precondition for arriving at "heavenly" experience.[18]

But what are the capabilities of the look? What kind of agency does the prisoner lose when he is led out of the cave and into the region above? In "Plato's Doctrine of Truth," Heidegger claims that Socrates' allegory of philosophical ascent "recounts a story of passages from one dwelling place to another" (168). Each of these dwelling places provides the locus for the partial unveiling of Being (168–72). This unveiling happens independently of the human look. It is not the product of vision, but rather, the "fundamental trait of [B]eing itself" (179).

It is my contention that the story Socrates tells in the parable of the cave is in a number of respects the exact opposite of the one Heidegger finds there. The central drama of book 7 of the *Republic* is concealment, rather than revelation. What is concealed is not Being, but rather the world itself. This is not to say, however, that Being has no part to play in this drama. On the contrary, Being is precisely what the world loses when it is eclipsed in this way. Darkness precipitates the loss of Being because it is only insofar as creatures and things appear that they can Be.[19] Finally, it is we alone who determine whether the world will appear, and so Be, or languish in the darkness of non-Being. We bring things into the light by looking, in the strongest and most important sense of that word. We conceal them when we fail to look in this way: when we neglect to exercise the visual agency with which our subjectivity entrusts us.

I am clearly not imputing the same meaning to "Being" that Socrates does. "Being" signifies for me not "truth" or "reality," but rather that "more-than-reality" with which phenomenal forms shine when they are allowed to appear. It is the capacity to irradiate in this way—the power to confer something far greater than life or death—of which the look is divested when it turns from the visible to the invisible.

ECLIPSING THE WORLD

Because the world of phenomenal forms figures in the parable of the cave only as a realm of deceptive shadows, the reader of that text easily loses sight of what the turn to the Good implies. Fortunately, the *Symposium*[20]—another of the middle Socratic dialogues—clarifies the stakes. In this dialogue, Socrates accounts for the exemplary spectator's upward journey as the climbing of a ladder leading from earthly to heavenly beauty.[21] On the lowest rung, this spectator looks at the beauty of an individual body. Then comes the beauty of all bodies; the beauty of the soul; the beauty of activities and laws; the beauty of every kind of knowledge; and finally that universal beauty which is synonymous with the Good.[22] For the spectator who climbs this ladder all the way to the top, beauty is freed from the vicissitudes of time. It becomes an "everlasting loveliness which neither comes nor goes, which neither flowers nor fades" (211a). Beauty also becomes singular: the "same on every hand . . . now as then, here as there, [and] this way as that way." Finally, beauty becomes disembodied; it no longer consists of "a face, or of hands, or of anything that is of the flesh," and inheres neither in "words, nor knowledge, nor a something that exists in something else" (211a).[23]

At first, it seems as if the ladder represents beauty itself, in all of its manifold forms. The spectator presumably climbs it by lifting his eyes from one rung to the next. Before long, however, it becomes evident that the ladder is a metaphor for the process of sublimation and departicularization, to which the spectator himself subjects beauty. The central topic of the *Symposium* is love: what it is, where it comes from, to what it leads. And the most privileged prototype of the lover, advanced by this dialogue, is the one who gazes upon an abstract and spiritual beauty. Looking and loving are thus virtual synonyms in the *Symposium*.[24] Since one looks lovingly at an abstract and spiritual beauty only by looking away from the world, it can only be through a libidinal withdrawal from phenomenal forms that one climbs the ladder described by Socrates. Not surprisingly, then, at the moment that the protagonist of his story succeeds in abstracting beauty away from individual bodies, he realizes that "this wild gaping after just one body is a small thing," to be despised (210b).[25]

Although I used the words "libidinal withdrawal" a moment ago to indicate the action that makes possible each stage of this spectator's ascent, these words in fact accurately characterize only what occurs at the site of the viewing subject. Something rather different occurs at the site of what is seen; when Socrates' spectator withdraws his affect from a particular visual object, it undergoes a radical diminution. This is because this spectator climbs his metaphoric ladder by means of a sustained *Aufhebung*, or sublation: by lifting beauty up and out of what permits him to see it until it no longer has any earthly locus. Since he reaches the top of the ladder only by performing this sublation in relation to all earthly forms, he might be said to arrive at the Good only by rendering the whole world barren and poor.

In the *Phaedrus*, another dialogue centrally concerned with the journey toward the Good, Socrates again depicts the exemplary spectator as a lover. Here, this lover is not obliged to renounce all corporeal beauty; some concessions are made to the affection most of us entertain for a particular body. However, what Socrates gives with one hand he takes away with the other.[26] The only kinds of erotic bonds he sanctions are those which serve to remind us of what we would otherwise forget: the nonsensual spectacle of that "mystery" which is the "most blessed of all."[27] Such recollection is, moreover, at its most exemplary when it abstracts away from the body in which ideal beauty has been incarnated to ideal beauty itself.[28] Socrates tells Phaedrus that the "experience" of the lover is properly "beyond [his] comprehension because [he] cannot fully grasp what it is that [he is] seeing" (250a–b). The lover is also ideally disembodied, or "beside [himself]"(250a).

As these last words indicate, the *Phaedrus*—like the *Republic* and the *Symposium*—stresses the deindividuation to which the nonsensory spectacle of the Beautiful subjects the one who gazes upon it. It is not only the one whom the lover loves, but also the lover himself who comes to function as the mirror of a higher beauty (255b–e).[29] Moreover, the rapture with which the loved one beholds this reflection of beauty is communicated to him by the lover himself; Socrates—with surprising candor about its damaging potentiality—compares it to "an eye disease [which comes] from someone else" (255d). Finally, as I indicated above, at the moment at which the lover beholds the "ultimate vision" of beauty, his look, too, conforms to what it sees (250c). This deindividuation of the look represents a crucial feature of the process through which Socrates negates phenomenal forms. This is because it is in the *particularity* of the human eye that its transfigurative properties reside. It is only by assuming its utmost "ownness" that the look can make the world shine—only by becoming *itself* that it can deliver other creatures and things into *their* Being.[30]

Although the *Phaedrus*, like the *Symposium* and the *Republic*, finally makes little provision for the pleasure entailed in looking at the unique beauty of a particular body, it does acknowledge the intensity of that pleasure. Such beauty induces "madness," "yearning," "joy," and the "sweetest of all pleasures" in the soul of the one who gazes upon it, who is "not at all willing to give [it] up" (251d, e). The *Phaedrus* also associates love of the world with a desire that cannot be satisfied—with a yearning that becomes only more achingly intense over time (251a–e, 252a–b). It seems that such beauty "reflects back at us that of which our eyes will never have their fill," as Walter Benjamin would say.[31]

The *Phaedrus* includes as well two passages detailing the dramatically different pleasure provided by celestial contemplation. The emphasis throughout these passages is upon the wholeness, unity, completion, fullness, and satisfaction which divine loveliness brings to the one who looks at it (247c–e and 250b–c). Not only is the Form of Beauty "perfect," "simple," and "unshakeable," but those who celebrate it are also "wholly perfect and free of all . . . troubles" (250c). It seems to heal all wounds, make good all inadequacies, fill all voids.

The distinction that Socrates draws in the *Phaedrus* between world spectatorship and its celestial counterpart helps us to understand something crucial about each of them. The world spectator is emphatically a desiring subject. He has done more than accede to lack; he has learned to take pleasure in his own insatiability. He derives pleasure from his own nonsatisfaction because he knows that it, and not the Good invoked by Socrates in the *Republic*, is the wellspring of beauty. The kind of disembodied vision celebrated by the middle Socratic dialogues represents, on the contrary, the end of desire. The protagonist of the parable of the cave does not remain at this zero point of subjectivity; he is obliged by those who lead him out of the cave to return to it once more.[32] Nevertheless, the *Republic*, like the *Phaedrus* and the *Symposium*, is saturated with longing for it. This desire for the end of desire, which is finally the motor force behind all metaphysics, does more than attest to an incapacity to tolerate any pleasure other than that of satiety; it also comes uncannily close to approximating that pure *destrudo* about which Freud speaks in *The Ego and the Id*.[33]

CREATION STORIES (I)

In book 7 of the *Republic*, Socrates describes the Good as the "cause" of all visible things (516c). In the *Timaeus*, a dialogue which purports to take place the day after the end of the dialogue on which the *Republic* is based (17b–19b) and in which Socrates is a tacitly approving listener,[34] Timaeus describes how the Demiurge created the world. Because the *Timaeus* begins with a recapitulation of part of the argument from the *Republic*, and because it too makes reference to the Forms, its creation story seems to come as an elaboration of the terms under which the Good "caus[ed]" the visible. However, Timaeus's narrative contradicts book 7 of the *Republic* in several important respects.

First, unlike Socrates' account of divine causation in the *Republic*, Timaeus's creation story features both a paternal principle and a maternal principle. Timaeus's paternal principle is equivalent to what Plato metaphorizes as the Forms in the *Republic*. It is the agency through which the Demiurge—whose more abstract structural counterpart in the *Republic* is, I would argue, the Good—creates the universe. However, the maternal principle is matter. And, whereas Timaeus stresses the shape-giving and propagative properties of the paternal principle, he emphasizes the receptive and absorptive properties of matter. The maternal principle is devoid of any intrinsic formal qualities; it is purely receptive, assuming whatever form is imposed upon it by the paternal principle. "For the moment, we need to keep in mind three types of things," says Timaeus:

> that which comes to be, that in which it comes to be, and that after which the thing coming to be is modeled, and which is the source of its coming to be. It is in fact appropriate to compare the receiving thing to a mother, the source to a father, and the nature between them to their offspring. We also must understand that if the imprints are to be varied, with all the varieties there to see, this thing upon which the imprints are to be formed could not be well prepared for that role if it were not itself devoid of any of those characters that it is to receive from elsewhere. For if it resembled any of the things that enter it, it could not successfully copy their opposites or things of a totally different nature whenever it were to receive them. It would be showing its own face as well. This is why the thing that is to receive in itself all the elemental kinds must be totally devoid of any characteristics. . . . We [can] speak of it as an invisible and characterless sort of thing, one that receives all things and shares in a most perplexing way in what is intelligible, a thing extremely difficult to comprehend. (50c–51b)

Although this passage poses a clear challenge to the principles of oneness[35] and form-giving upon which Socrates places so much emphasis in the *Republic*, it at least leaves unchallenged the ultimate primacy of the paternal principle. However, when we cross-reference this passage with book 7 of the *Republic*, a more disconcerting possibility emerges. In the parable of the cave, Socrates claims that the world does not consist of faithful replicas of the Good, as Timaeus suggests in the passage I have just quoted, but rather of base simulacra, degraded or insufficient copies (514a–c and 532b–c). He thereby imputes to the created world a divergence from the paternal principle or Forms that only an insubordinate maternal principle could explain. It looks from the vantage point of this earlier text as if the maternal principle is not mere putty in the hands of the paternal principle, but rather a force in its own right. Indeed, the parable of the cave raises the possibility that it is finally the maternal principle and not the paternal principle which gives rise to all visible things.

Luce Irigaray makes these troubling discrepancies and cross-references between the *Timaeus* and the *Republic* the basis for an alternate account of creation, and one which will help us go further in our postmetaphysical reading of the parable of the cave. In *Speculum of the Other Woman*, she suggests that because the mother/matter is herself lacking in any sense of propriety, she cannot help but corrupt any form that is imposed upon her. She lends herself to the production only of "bad" copies: of copies that travesty what they imitate.[36] The maternal principle is also unfaithful even to these degraded forms. She may be "a clean slate ready"[37] for at least some version of "the father's impressions," but that slate can be immediately wiped clean so as to be ready for a new impression. "Unstable, inconsistent, fickle, unfaithful," Irigaray writes, "she seems ready to receive all beings into herself. Keeping no trace of them. Without memory" (307).

Irigaray also evacuates the father from the position of Demiurge, and installs the mother in his place. She does so by showing that the paternal principle cannot be the source of the world, as Timaeus claims. The Forms are opposed to "all change, all alteration or modification—optical, directional, or semantic" (320); they maintain themselves in an eternal sameness. They are also unified under a higher agency, which—regardless of whether it is represented as the Good, as is the case in the *Republic*, or as the Demiurge, as is the case in the *Timaeus*—cannot logically be posited as the source of all of the material and perspectival multiplicity with which Plato associates the phenomenal domain in the first of those texts. The only way of accounting for the creation of the world is through a contrary principle—one given over to multiplicity, mutability, and formal innovation. This contrary principle is ready at hand: it is, of course, the mother/matter.

The alternative creation story which Irigaray teases out of the parable of the cave might seem to be true to this text in at least one sense: it, too, encourages us to turn around, to face our origin (245). However, by "origin" Irigaray means not the sun, but rather the strange scene at the back of the cave. It is, moreover, not so easy to say what facing this origin would entail. Irigaray tells us that the nether shadows that represent the world in Plato's parable "demand a complexity of time and tenses for their production" (287). We will never understand them, it seems, so long as we insist upon telling the story of creation as a chronological narrative, in which the copy follows the original.

The author of *Speculum of the Other Woman* is also apparently faithful to the parable of the cave in one other respect: like Plato, she associates the domain of appearance with shadows, copies, fakes, simulacra, mirror images, and other forms of traditionally despised seeming (246). However, unlike Socrates, Irigaray does not hesitate to impute truth to such visual forms. The truth which interests her is apparently not that which is to be found by gazing heavenward, but rather that which creatures and things assume only when they are allowed to refer to something beyond themselves—to become, in effect, representations. As Irigaray puts it at one point in a section called "Plato's *Hystera*," "let us give exclusive privilege to the fake, the mask, the fantas[m], because, at least at times, they mark the nostalgia we feel for something even more true" (269).

I am fascinated by Irigaray's reading of Timaeus's "invisible and characterless" thing, which—although itself devoid of properties and resistant to every predication—nevertheless provides the basis for all appearance. With her analysis of the mother/matter, Irigaray challenges the primacy not only of the principles of oneness and form-giving, but also those of reason and knowledge. She substitutes for the category of a prime mover, both so rational and so self-present as to be synonymous with intelligibility itself, something which is finally less a thing than a blind but potent drive toward an ever changing manifestation. Since this endlessly mutating materiality is, moreover, itself shaped and defined by the forms that it assumes, it cannot help but challenge our usual ways of conceptualizing causality. Here, what causes is itself determined by what it causes.

However, by characterizing this nonfoundational foundation as "maternal," Irigaray seems to confer upon it some identity of its own, and thereby to undermine everything that is most radical about it. Irigaray also fails to locate what is in my view the real site of productive "nothingness" in the parable of the cave: it is in light rather than matter that we will find this text's generative principle. I hasten to add that this does not mean giving priority to the metaphoric sun in the parable. The notion of sun worship is as inimical to me as it is to Irigaray.

CREATION STORIES (2)

In his seventh seminar,[38] Lacan advances another creation story, and one which may better help us rise to the challenge of reading the *Republic* and the *Timaeus* together. Like Timaeus's creation story, Lacan's features a mysterious nonentity which, although itself devoid of any essential defining attributes, is capable of assuming an infinitude of visual forms. And Lacan's creation story, too, attributes to this nonentity a generative force. This prime mover is what Lacan calls *das Ding*, the impossible nonobject of desire. It is that which each of us must sacrifice in order to become a subject, that whose loss makes it possible for other beings to matter to us. Although *das Ding* is often metaphorically conflated with the mother, it is finally neither maternal nor paternal.[39] Lacan also associates it less with matter than with radiance. It is to this that we owe our capacity to "light up" the world.[40]

It might seem that I am doing no more here than rehearsing an argument already made familiar by Freud in *Beyond the Pleasure Principle*:[41] since the backward path leading to complete satisfaction is blocked, we have no choice but to go forward, displacing affect away from the first, prohibited object of desire—which is classically the mother, but need not be—onto other, substitute objects. These subsequent objects owe their value to the fact that they are the recipients of what really belongs to the originary object. "Light" would then seem to be another name for the value inhering in whatever is first loved, and displacement something like the transport of a candle lit in this primal flame to ever more remote territories.

In fact, although Lacan also maintains that it is only through being the recipient of displacement away from a prior term that something can assume psychic value, his account of desire is in other respects very different from the Freudian one. *Das Ding* is not what we first desire. It becomes an object of desire only in its absence, and only as a result of a retroactive symbolization—through its incarnation in the form of subsequent actual objects of desire. Prior to its loss, *das Ding* is completely unspecifiable; it has neither properties nor attributes. It is something like "brute presence," a meaningless "*hic et nunc*," as Lacan puts it in the Rome discourse.[42] It is also irrecoverable as such. If, then, as in the Freudian account, we have no choice but to go forward, this is not merely because the backward path is blocked. It is, in addition, because there is nothing to return to—because no primally lost object awaits us.

There are also two other pressing reasons why the backward path ostensibly leading to satisfaction might finally be said to lead nowhere. First, to recover the here and now would be to annihilate ourselves as subjects. The thick atmosphere of spatial and temporal presence would not only be oppressive, but also libidinally lethal. Only through an ever renewed symbolization do we constitute and secure ourselves as subjects of desire. Second, we must go forward rather than backward because our doing so is the condition for the world to appear and so to Be, in the strongest and most important sense of that word.

"In the beginning was the Word, which is to say, the signifier," Lacan remarks at one point in *Seminar VII* (213). Although he might seem to be referring here to the biblical account of creation, in which God's words precipitate the world, the speech act to which he attributes an originary value is finally less verbal than libidinal.[43] It is also conducive not so much of existence as of that more-than-reality which Socrates calls "beauty." We confer this gift of beauty when we allow other people and things to incarnate the impossible nonobject of desire—when we permit them to embody what is itself without body, to make visible what is itself invisible.

Many subjects are unwilling to exercise their creative potentiality—to exchange their "being" for the world's Being. They seek instead to close down the void whose opening is synonymous with subjectivity. As is no doubt evident by now, Socrates' exemplary spectator stands for all such subjects. In making the journey out of the cave and into the realm outside, this spectator might be said to succumb to the siren call of *das Ding*. He yields to the temptation which is always strong in all of us to retreat from the ache of lack and the ardors of desire into a fullness and plenitude of being. To do so ostensibly means to turn away from all of the creatures and things which have ever shone with indirect light to the source of light itself. However, what it really means is to push these creatures and things out of the sphere of illumination, and back again into obscurity.

Socrates' spectator does not hesitate to lay violent hands upon other beings in this way; they are, he tells himself, mere substitutes and surrogates, pale copies of eternal beauty. In fact, though, the radiance he seeks can only be seen in an indirect form. Indeed, it *exists* only in that form, because it is created not through the presence, but rather through the absence of the metaphoric sun. This light is also not something he can possess, but only something he can impart. Before he can see it, he must bestow it.

It should be clear by now that what Socrates calls the "Good" is in fact radically evil. One accedes to it only through the most extreme form of destruction imaginable: through the undoing of appearance. It is, moreover, not in the final realization of a "pure shining" that the pleasure he celebrates inheres. Were we ever to complete the journey which Socrates describes in the parable of the cave, we would discover not radiance, but darkness; not Being, but the blank meaninglessness of the here and now. The only *jouissance* which we would encounter on our long journey away from phenomenal forms would be the ecstasy of a pure annihilation.[44]

CREATION STORIES (3)

The parable of the cave itself anticipates the argument I have just elaborated in several surprising ways. In an important passage at the end of book 6 of the *Republic*, Plato defines the sun as "the offspring of the good, which the good begot as its analogue" (508b). This is what might be called (following Stanley Fish) a "self-consuming utterance."[45] In characterizing the sun as the *offspring* of the Good, Plato imputes to the Good both chronological priority and the status of origin. In describing the sun as the *analogue* of the Good, however, he establishes a relation between the two which is a-diachronic. As we have learned from Lacan, there is no time within the imaginary, locus of all specular or analogic relations.[46]

In book 7 of the *Republic*, Socrates affirms once again at the manifest level of his argument the chronological priority of the Good over the sun, as well as the determining relation of the one to the other (517b–c). However, in what might be called the "performance" of his argument, effect precedes cause; the visible order comes first and gives form to the intelligible. Moreover, Socrates never succeeds in rectifying this perverse chronology; throughout book 7 of the *Republic*, he always encourages us to apprehend the Good in the guise of the sun, rather than the sun in the guise of the Good. After the prisoner climbs out of the cave of the world, and into the sphere beyond, it is also—in an uncanny return of the same—precisely the phenomenal forms of our earthly habitation that he once again encounters. It seems that there is no getting beyond the earth and heavens. Finally, after obliging the prisoner to get up from his seat in the cave, and to embark upon the regressive journey toward the ostensible cause of all that is, Socrates surprisingly turns him around and sends him back to the cave.

Socrates' Good thus has all of the temporal complexity of Lacan's *das Ding*: it represents the origin, but it is constituted as such only through a posteriori symbolization. Furthermore, any attempt to recover this lost origin by reversing the process of symbolization is doomed to failure. There is no Good to be found on the other side of the sun, and it is with the utmost difficulty that the prisoner even succeeds in raising his eyes to that celestial body. Finally, the parable of the cave begins as it ends: with world spectatorship. If we continue to read Plato today, over a century since the publication of *The Gay Science*, it is at least in part because of this.

CREATION STORIES (4)

When others look at us from a perspective other than the one from which we are accustomed to regard ourselves, we generally accuse them of not seeing us properly, or even of not allowing us to be ourselves. We experience every visual "augmentation" as an unconscionable colonization or subordination. I am working with a very different set of visual assumptions here. It is my view that were others to look at us through our own eyes, "ourselves" is precisely what we would never be. We can appear, and so Be, only if others "light" us up. To be lit up means to be seen from a vantage point from which we can never see ourselves. It also means to embody not our own, but rather *someone else's* idea of beauty. Our "essence" is thus strangely nonessential.

But this does not mean that the look has the right to dispose freely of the world. It is as important to grasp what the look cannot or should not do as to understand what it can do. Yet another story of creation can be of assistance to us in this respect—that provided in the first book of the Bible. This originary narrative—which Lacan himself invokes more than once in *Seminar VII*[47]—depicts God performing two different acts of symbolization, one of which arrogates to itself powers which exceed both the capacities and appropriate limits of the signifier, whether verbal or visual; and one of which is exemplary to a surprising degree of world spectatorship.

The opening verses of Genesis give powerful expression to the fantasy of creating out of nothing. God says "Let there be light," and for the first time ever, there is light;[48] "Let there be a dome in the midst of the waters, and let it separate the waters from the waters" (1.6), and water and sky are immediately separated from one another. Divine speech erupts out of nowhere, and creates everything that is. This account of the creation of the world provides the most striking example imaginable of the "sovereign performative"—of the performative which does precisely and punctually what it says, without previous authorization or precedent. It completely denies the reality of language as we know it: that we are as much spoken by language as speakers of it; that our only semiotic freedom is in the recontextualization and reconfiguration of what has already been said; that our utterances are always carried away from us; that not every performative performs what it intends.[49] The biblical story of creation also represents the most extreme instantiation of the will to power in the history of metaphysics.

But the first chapter of Genesis distinguishes clearly and decisively between the act of bringing into existence and the act of looking. Seeing plays no role in the summoning forth of the cosmos out of nothing. The divine look comes into play only subsequently, and says "yes" to the world. God looks at what he has created—at what already *is*—and "[sees] that it [is] good" (1.3). This account of the look encourages us to understand appearance outside the parameters of the sovereign performative. From it, we learn that the look is not omnipotent. It cannot do exactly as it wishes, without prior authorization or precedent. Nor can it create the world; to make is no more its province than to negate. The look can only conjure forth beauty where there is already being. This is, moreover, not a one-sided action. The being whom I light up with the radiance of affirmation supplies me with the form which allows me to see what I could not otherwise see; it alone makes possible beauty's embodiment. It is together, then, that we bring about its appearance.

A subsequent chapter of Genesis provides at least the provocation for conceptualizing appearance as an event which is also *initiated* from the side of the spectacle, rather than from that of the look. However, it obliges us to conceptualize this transaction outside all of our existing psychoanalytic and philosophical parameters. What has been created, we learn in this chapter, must now be symbolized. For that purpose God brings all of the animals and birds before Adam, to be named. Adam looks at each creature in turn and provides the appropriate word.

Because the naming of the animals and birds occurs prior to the Fall, it might seem to provide an example of prelapsarian speech—of words which are in a magical or continuous relation to things, not (like our own) disjunctive from or even antithetical to them. However, the verse in question suggests otherwise. It reads: "So out of the ground the Lord God formed every animal of the field and every bird of the air, and brought them to the man to see [לראות] what he would call them; and whatever the man called every living creature, that was its name" (2.19).

This attribution to God of the desire to *see* rather than to hear what names Adam will utter makes language referential of vision rather than of things themselves. It suggests that the function of words is not so much to describe the world within which we find ourselves, as to communicate to others how we see that world. Genesis 2.19 also intimates that God does not know in advance how Adam will see the animals which come before him. The same divine being who can conjure forth the universe with a few speech acts is apparently dependent upon words to gain access to the human look. This inexplicable failure of divine foreknowledge underscores the absolute singularity of vision. Even before the Fall, it seems, what each pair of eyes saw was unique to it alone.

At the same time that Genesis 2.19 foregrounds the subjectivity of the look, it gives the perceptual stimulus chronological priority over Adam's act of symbolization. It is only after an animal or bird has been displayed to Adam, it tells us, that he is able to utter that being's name.[50] What the Bible says about God can consequently also be said in a very precise way about Adam: he too must see what he will call the creatures which are brought before him. The authors of Genesis also maintain that the word which Adam speaks when he sees each animal or bird *is* that being's name.

While giving the lie to the notion that before the Fall language participated in the existential reality of the things they designated, this verse of Genesis helps us to understand that our symbolizations of creatures and things nevertheless properly come as a response to their very specific visual appeal. At the same time, what the world solicits from us is not an objective, but rather a subjective response. Creatures and things invite us to answer their appeal in a manner which, although fully responsive to their formal coordinates, is absolutely particular to ourselves. And only in doing so can we, like Adam, speak the word which names.

INSIDE THE CAVE

If the prisoner who is released from his ostensible bonds and dragged out of the cave in the *Republic* could be said to "unlook" the world, the companions he leaves behind would seem to provide us with at least a provisional model for thinking further about world spectatorship. Their companion's disappearance from the cave in no way deflects them from the activity which preoccupies them: looking at and speculating about the things of this world. Even after the ostensibly enlightened prisoner returns to the cave and presumably informs them about the intelligible region above,[51] they refuse to abandon this world for a supposedly better one (516e–517a). They seem convinced of the importance of what they are doing.

What—beyond the necessity for an unwavering commitment to the mundane—can we learn about world spectatorship from these figures? First of all, Plato suggests that the prisoners communicate verbally to each other about what they see (515b);[52] as in

Genesis, language seems to provide a vehicle for "looking" at other people's looks. At least within Arendt's retelling of the parable of the cave, moreover, this translation of vision into words would seem to constitute a social imperative, since each of the prisoners sees something different. Arendt defines the images on the wall as the spectators' *doxai*—"what and how things appear to them" (94). Earlier in the same essay, she intimates that while the "what" in these *doxai* may be common to all the prisoners, the "how" is heavily individuated. For the Greeks the notion of *doxa* "comprehended the world as it opens itself to me," and the assumption was that "the world opens up differently to every man, according to his position in it" (80).

These perspectival differences seem to constitute a permanent and accepted state of affairs. The prisoners are not working their way toward unanimity; nor do they dream of a moment at which it will finally be possible to adjudicate in some final way between their divergent perspectives on the cave/world. Rather, they seem to accept and revel in their perspectival differences. As Arendt puts it at one point, they "love seeing for its own sake, independent from all practical needs" (96). Their scopic divergences provide the basis and raison d'être for their social interaction.

The world spectator necessarily looks from his specific vantage point because that is the only site at which affirmation is possible. Heidegger suggests both in *History of the Concept of Time* and *Being and Time* that the constitutive state of human beings is to be "in-the-world."[53] Although this is a universal human condition, it is also always highly particular. Each human being occupies a specific *da*, or "there": it is a *Dasein*, or "there-being."[54] Although Heidegger provides no warrant for doing so, I will be arguing in the chapters that follow that the "there" from which each of us looks is finally semiotic; it represents the unique language of desire through which it is given to the subject to symbolize the world. Although each of us enters desire the same way, through the production of a psychic void, the process of specifying the beauty which is thereby produced is always strongly individuated. The constellation of recollections memorializing all of the embodiments of beauty which a given subject has made possible also provides a kind of "grammar" according to which he can care[55] about new beings and things. Every act of visual affirmation thus occurs not only via the incarnation of a formless and unspecifiable nonobject of desire, but also via the visual *reincarnation* of previous incarnations.

This is of course not how we normally look at other beings. Even when we succeed in focusing our vision upon this world, instead of some ostensibly truer sphere, and manage to avoid arrogating to ourselves the power to create it, we do not usually really *see* it. Rather, we treat other beings as if they were graspable and knowable objects, standing before us: as if they were "present-at-hand."[56] We do not allow other beings to appear because we are not "ourselves." Although none of us ever ceases to occupy a singular vantage point in the world, we are for the most part psychically displaced in relation to it. We are absorbed in the "they," in a relation of forgetfulness to ourselves.[57]

When we are lost in the "they," not only are we not "ourselves," but we also prevent others from becoming "themselves." At such moments, we could be said to be care-less of others. But the relation between ourselves and the world should not be thought in terms of cause and effect; we do not first embrace our "thereness," and then care for others. Rather, we become ourselves by caring for others. Arendt clarifies this principle with admirable precision in her Augustine book. As she makes clear, she learned it from Augustine himself, one of her earliest intellectual love-objects: "Since man is not self-sufficient and therefore always desires something outside himself, the question of who he is can only be resolved by the object of his desire . . . : 'Such is each as is his love.'"[58] Once again we are obliged to conceptualize "essence" in a profoundly nonessential way.[59]

The parable of the cave is of invaluable assistance to us in clarifying what separates world spectatorship not only from the spiritual kind of vision celebrated by Plato, but also from more everyday kinds of looking. Those who are most skilled at the shadow

game, we learn in the *Republic*, are those who are "sharpest at iden-
tifying the shadows as they [pass] by and who best [remember]
which usually [come] earlier, which later, and which simultaneously, and who [can] thus best divine the future" (516c–d). They are
those who look to the future in expectation of finding the past.

The "there" which each of us inhabits is finally as much temporal as spatial. Indeed, strange as it may sound, it is only through
a particular relation to time that *Dasein* assumes its place in the
world. It is for this reason that the same philosopher who defines
the human being as a "there-being" does not hesitate to say of
Dasein that it "*is time itself.*"[60] The time which each of us might be
said to be is our past, which does not so much "follo[w] along after" us, as "g[o] ahead" of us.[61] This time, I will be arguing, is finally the time of our desire. It both persists, in the guise of a kind
of language, and insists, in the form of what we are at any moment
tending-toward. But it is only when we not merely grasp ourselves
as the speakers of this language, but also learn to deploy it as the
agency for disclosing other creatures and things, that we make our
time our own, and so assume our "there." The world spectator is
consequently not just someone to whom the past returns, but
someone who holds himself open to the new form it will take—
who anticipates and affirms the transformative manifestation of
what was in what is.

So far, I have described the parable of the cave as if it were an
allegory only about the singularity of the look. In fact, Socrates represents the kind of looking which facilitates appearance as a *plurality* of looks.[62] Whereas the prisoner who "escapes" from the cave effects a solitary journey toward the truth, only at that point to enter
into a form of vision which would be the same for every other truth
seeker, each of the prisoners who remains behind might be said to
realize his distinctiveness only within the parameters of a collectivity. How are we to understand this emphasis upon a scopic plurality?

First, it is crucial that the perspectives from which the world
can be seen be as many as possible. The more singular vantage
points from which something is looked at, the richer is the Being

into which it is inducted. And the more individual outlooks there are upon the world, the greater are the chances for each and every being within it to be lit up by at least one look. In *The Gay Science*, Nietzsche commits himself to the defiantly antimetaphysical undertaking of world affirmation. He dreams of devoting himself to this project in a limitless way—of affirming everything that is, no matter how pitiful, ugly, or terrifying. But he finds this an impossible undertaking; sometimes, he confesses, he must look away (223). There is no living being of whom this is not true. None of us is capable of finding everything that he sees beautiful. Every one of us performs many times every day the *Aufhebung* described by Plato's Diotima, lifting the idea of loveliness up and out of certain bodies.[63] The affirmative look is therefore by very definition a collective look, with each pair of eyes making good where some other pair fails.

It is also crucial for the functioning of the look itself that there be other looks. As long as we view a being from a single standpoint, even when that standpoint is our very own, we cannot help but substantialize it. In order to release a creature or thing into its Being, we must apprehend it in its perspectival diversity. This does not mean that we should strive in all our visual transactions with that being to take account of all of the possible perspectives from which it could be seen. Such a totality is an impossibility, since the perspectives which would constitute something in its full Being are infinite. It is, moreover, vital for creatures and things that they always remain partially concealed; concealment provides protection as well as obscurity.[64] What is crucial, rather, is that each of us comes to understand our look in its specificity and partialness. The parable of the cave suggests that it is by listening to others speak that we can gain access to a position from which this might be possible.

When we take into account not only the singularity, but also the plurality of world spectatorship, we are able to understand another way in which it is informed by temporality. The collective looking which makes appearance possible does not ever occur "all at once." It unfolds over time, with one look challenging, corroborating, undoing, or extending what other looks have seen before. Being thus eludes totalization not only in space but also in time. In fact, as should by now be clear, Being is a becoming. And this becoming does not achieve stabilization even with death. Long after a given being has ceased to be physically in the world, it remains there, mnemonically, "housed" in all of the psyches that have ever affirmed it. In each of those psyches, it is not a coherent and stable entity, but a constellation of diverse and highly particularized sounds and images, caught up in a ceaseless process of flux and transformation.

BETWEEN PSYCHOANALYSIS
AND PHILOSOPHY

As the reader has no doubt remarked, I have employed two seemingly incompatible vocabularies in this chapter: that of philosophy and that of psychoanalysis. I have spoken at moments about the importance of allowing beings to enter into their Being, and at others about subjectivity, desire, and memory. Heidegger is insistent upon specifying Being in nonpsychic terms. Psychoanalysis, on the other hand, has never been willing to pose what William J. Richardson calls "the Being-question."[65] Who or what "authorizes" me to mix the two vocabularies in this way?

The answer is of course no one and nothing. In situating myself between psychoanalysis and philosophy, rather than safely inside one or the other, I have left myself without the usual discursive sanctions. I am thus obliged to acknowledge what I might otherwise disavow: my discourse is as groundless as desire itself. What I have to offer is only what can be seen from the finite and singular perspective that this vantage point opens up. Others will be able to apprehend what I cannot apprehend: the many perspectives which mine works to close off.

It appears to me, from the site of my "betweenness," that the word "subject" cannot be reserved for those human beings who apprehend the world in an objectifying way, as Heidegger maintains in "The Age of the World Picture" and "A Question Concerning Technology."[66] It is a concept without which even the most "authentic" forms of *Dasein* cannot be fully understood. The assumption by a human being of its "in the worldness" is something which must take place at the site of subjectivity. All of the key concepts through which Heidegger conceptualizes this condition in his early writing—Being-towards-death, thrownness, repetition, care—are in my view psychically specific, and will be correspondingly treated here.

But if philosophy needs psychoanalysis to clarify the psychic conditions of *Dasein*, psychoanalysis also badly needs the challenge which this latter notion poses to its thinking. The concept of *Dasein* makes visible something which psychoanalysis has functioned to make invisible: what it means for the world that each one of us is in it. Heidegger suggests at the end of "What Is Metaphysics?" that the basic question of metaphysics is: "Why are there beings at all, and why not rather nothing?"[67] He maintains that it is only by confronting the possibility of this nothing that we can move beyond beings to Being. Psychoanalysis also needs to makes this project its own. Since Lacan, those of us working within that discourse have begun to understand that subjectivity pivots around a void: that each of us is in a sense no-thing.[68] However, we have not learned to hear the call to Being which echoes out of this void. We have not yet understood that the "no-thing" links us inextricably to the world we inhabit, and makes its affairs ours as well.

2

EATING THE BOOK

We have grown accustomed in recent years to conceptualizing subjectivity prepositionally. We think of ourselves as subjects "of" language, "of" discourse, and "of" ideology. The subject who is the concern of this book is also propositional: she is "in" the world. But I do not mean this preposition to be as immediately intelligible as the others have come to seem. We are not in the world merely by virtue of being born into it; indeed, most of us are not really in the world at all. Paradoxical as it may sound, we are only really in the world when it is in us—when we have made room within our psyches for it to dwell and expand. The preposition "in" is thus in this case less spatial than affective.

Freud's Schreber case history is generally read as his primary contribution to the theorization of paranoia. What we tend to overlook is that this text also represents one of psychoanalysis's most important disquisitions on the interdependence of world and psyche. Freud describes Schreber's illness as the failure of his capacity to love—as the withdrawal "from the people in his environment and from the external world generally of the libidinal cathexis which he ha[d] hitherto directed on to them." As a result, "everything has become indifferent and irrelevant to him."[1] But Freud does not stop here. As if to make evident that there is more at issue in the case of Schreber than a lonely psyche, he underscores that figure's own sense that a great "catastrophe" is imminent: the end of the world as such. Freud also provides by way of a commentary upon this state of affairs the following quotation from Goethe's *Faust*, thereby attributing to Schreber's subjective state a surprising effectivity with respect to the larger environment:

> Woe! Woe!
> Thou hast it destroyed,
> The beautiful world,
> With powerful fist!
> In ruins 'tis hurled,
> By the blow of a demigod shattered! . . .
> Mightier
> For the children of men,
> More splendid
> Build it again,
> In thine own bosom build it anew! (70)[2]

The point here is not that the world does not exist in reality unless it exists for us subjectively. We do not possess the capacity to confer or withdraw being. Our power is both greater and lesser: we determine whether other creatures and things will continue to languish in the darkness of concealment, or whether they will enter into the light of Being. We determine, that is, whether or not they can *appear*. And, as Freud suggests through Goethe, we do so by either providing or failing to provide the open space within which they can emerge. The names for this space are many. Goethe, as we have seen, calls it "breast." Heidegger prefers "clearing," and Lacan "*manque-à-être*."

Goethe's anatomical metaphor will have no further role to play here. However, the concepts of the clearing and of *manque-à-être* will both figure prominently in the pages that follow. It will, indeed, be by moving back and forth between Heidegger and Lacan that I will attempt to theorize what it means for us to be the site of the world's disclosure.

'DASEIN'

Dasein is Heidegger's word for what I call the subject. Heidegger himself, however, would object strenuously to my use of the latter word. He reserves it for a historically specific form of human beingness, one to which Descartes gives rise with the *Discourse on Method* and the *Meditations on First Philosophy*, and which finds its fullest realization in Nietzsche's writings. The subject is Heidegger's name for those who seek to objectify the world through representation—for those who attempt to master it epistemologically, and thereby make of themselves the relational center of all that is. The subject is pure will-to-power.[3]

Whatever objections we might raise to this highly idiosyncratic definition of "subject," we must be grateful to Heidegger for the conceptual reconfiguration he effected in our thinking of human beingness when he gave preference instead to *Dasein*. *Dasein* signifies "existence" in everyday German, but this is not how Heidegger is using it. He means us to hear the literal meaning which that everyday meaning usually conceals: "there-being," or—to translate this into more idiomatic English, "being-there."[4] This is an astonishing formulation through which to refer to what we usually think of as a person, since the "being" in *Dasein* is a verbal rather than a nominal construction. Heidegger seems to be asking us to think human beingness outside the confines not only of philosophical, but also of grammatical subjectivity. He seems to be inviting us, that is, to conceptualize ourselves nonsubstantially, as an action rather than an entity.

What is this action? We do not generally think of "being" as an activity, even when it entails a locational condition. Indeed, grammarians are fond of telling us that the verb "to be" is "passive." To "be there" signifies in the first instance "to be in the world." For the Heidegger of *Being and Time*, that entails being "with" other human beings (155). It also entails being "alongside" things (155–56). One is "with" and "alongside," not so much spatially as in the mode of "care." Care can take many forms, including "having to do with something, producing something, attending to something and looking after it [. . .], undertaking, accomplishing, [exploring], interrogating, [observing], discussing, determining" (83).

It may not seem that this definition of *Dasein* brings us any closer to the domain of action. However, "to act" means something different for Heidegger than it customarily does. In "Letter to Humanism," he writes that "the essence of action is accomplishment," and that "to accomplish means to unfold something into the fullness of its essence, to lead it forth into this fullness."[5] This is precisely what we do when we care authentically or disclosively. On such occasions, we "*mak[e] room*" for other creatures and things.[6] We thereby allow what "proximally and for the most part does *not* show itself at all" to come into the light: to move from invisibility to visibility.[7]

Unfortunately, not all forms of caring are disclosive—not all allow other beings to "be encountered" in the way which is constitutive for appearance. This is because we are for the most part "with" other creatures and things in what *Being and Time* calls an "inauthentic" way (163–68).[8] We are absorbed with both as present-at-hand entities rather than as phenomena, which means—within the present discussion—that we substantialize or entify them.[9] We are able to do so because, when fallen, we are engrossed in the "they."

Being engrossed in the "they" encourages us to apprehend other beings as present-at-hand entities because it implies seeing them from one uniform standpoint. Absorption in the "they" encourages us to regard other creatures and things through those perceptual coordinates which are most emphatically and frequently reiterated in our culture, and which therefore interpose themselves almost automatically between us and the world—through what might be called the "given-to-be-seen."[10] Although we are at such inauthentic moments still in the world, we are not really "there."

Heidegger maintains in *Being and Time* that it is only "in temporalizing itself" that *Dasein* can properly be said to be "there" (417), and hence to have emerged in its full and always unique specificity. To be "in the world," in the most profound sense, thus means to be within temporality. Temporality is profoundly inimical to our usual notions of personhood, since it produces an ecstatic being—one who can claim to be only from a place it can never occupy, a place outside itself. As long as we live, we are not yet. There is always something outstanding, something determinative. The fateful event after which there will no longer be something outstanding, and after which the question of who we are will have been established, is of course death (276–77). However, with this event we will cease to exist. There is thus no moment when we properly "are." Our being must rather be defined in terms of what, from the moment of death, we will have been; it inheres in the future perfect.

Although our death thus exercises a decisive influence over the present, most of us live our entire lives in radical disavowal of it as an event to which we must succumb. Death, as Heidegger says, is something that happens only to other people.[11] This disavowal is fatal, since we thereby abjure one of the most important arenas within which our limited capacity for freedom can be exercised. In effect, *Being and Time* proposes that, although death will have the last word in determining who we will have been, it is possible for us to enter into a relation to that event which will permit us to participate in its metaphoric speech act:

If Dasein, by anticipation, lets death become powerful in itself, then, as free for Death, Dasein understands itself in its own *superior power*, the power of its finite freedom, so that in this freedom, which "is" only in its having chosen to make such a choice, it can take over the *powerlessness* of abandonment to its having done so, and can thus come to have a clear vision for the accidents of the Situation that has been disclosed. (436)

To "let death become powerful in itself" is to be "towards-death."[12] "Being-towards-death" is anticipatory; it orients the subject toward the future from which its present might be said to issue. It is also individuating. Death is that one moment when each of us is irreducibly alone; it is an event which we can share with no one, and of which no one can absolve us. Being-towards-death consequently isolates the subject from the "they" in which it has been previously absorbed. In so doing, it singularizes *Dasein* "down to itself" (308).

Being-towards-death not only orients us toward the future, it also focuses us upon the "situation" into which we have been "thrown" (346). This is another of the ways in which Being-towards-death individuates *Dasein*. For Heidegger, the word "situation" is primarily "factical";[13] it has to do with the concrete parameters of our Being-in-the-world. Although Heidegger does not say as much, the category "situation" would seem capable of accommodating such notions as a person's social, geographical, and economic circumstances, all of which circumscribe her possibilities. It could also be said that we are thrown into history and into language.[14]

"Thrownness" signifies in these respects, as in all others, "not being in control of one's basis or foundation." As Heidegger says in *Being and Time*, we can "*never* . . . have power over [our] ownmost Being from the ground up" (330). Like death, "thrownness" is thus a potent metaphor for finitude of all kind. And once again we marshal what might be called our "little freedom"[15] not when we attempt to escape these constraints, but rather when we "choose" them. By embracing our limits, we participate in the determination of what we will have been, and thereby transform them into a kind of agency.

It should be clear by now that the individuation that Being-towards-death makes possible has nothing whatever to do with any traditional notion of "personhood." For Heidegger, to grasp oneself as "thrownness into death" entails coming to terms with oneself as a "not," or a "nullity."[16] These signifiers suggest that human subjectivity or *Dasein* may be in a certain sense less about "being" than about "not being"—about "not being punctually in the present," "not being in control of death," "not being one's own ground," and so on.

How are we to think together the two attributes which Heidegger links to authentic *Dasein* or in-the-worldness: disclosive care, and Being-towards-death? *Being and Time* suggests that Being-towards-death not only isolates us from the "they," but also silences the empty speech through which the "they" manifests itself, either outside or inside us. In the ensuing silence, we are able to hear a call to which we have previously been deaf. This call comes from ourselves, and it summons us to ourselves. We hear it by experiencing a sense of guilt, or—as Heidegger sometimes puts it—by being ready to have a conscience. This guilt, however, has nothing to do with actual misdeeds, and it can never be exonerated. Rather, is our way of registering our limitless and finally ontological responsibility for, or indebtedness to,[17] other creatures and things. This is because the self to which we call ourselves at those moments that we are "towards-death" is the self of care.[18]

But what is the self of care? Within what subjective faculty do our disclosive powers reside? These questions can only be answered by broadening our understanding of *Dasein*'s "thrownness."

THROWNNESS

The situation into which each of us has been thrown is in certain respects broadly cultural and in other respects completely unique. Because Heidegger tends to oppose the individual to the collective, he makes it difficult to see how complexly the two are imbricated. In addition, because the concerns of psychoanalysis would appear to fall under the rubric of the "ontic" for Heidegger, and his own account of language and *Dasein* is instead insistently focused upon what he takes to be the ontological, he pays no attention to those aspects of *Dasein*'s "situatedness" that have the most explanatory value for any understanding of care: the entry into

language and the incest prohibition. In order to arrive at a sufficiently nuanced understanding of our in-the-worldness, it would
thus seem necessary to extend Heidegger's thought in some seemingly un-Heideggerian directions.

I suggested above that we are thrown not only into a certain social and economic situation, but also into language. As Jacques Lacan has taught us, to be thrown into language implies, first of all, to
be dependent for our meaning upon a linguistic system which is
there before we are born, will continue after we have died, and is in
every respect "bigger" than we are.[19] We can use this language only
to say what it allows us to say, and its rules govern how we must use
it. When we speak or write it, our words always say both more and
less than we intend. In all of these respects, language might be said
to speak us more than we speak it.[20]

We cannot single-handedly remake our language so that it better serves our needs. Nor can we substitute for this language one of
our own devising, since—to be a language—a verbal system must be
communicable. Finally, we cannot use language to say what things
"are." Words derive their meanings from their relationships to
other words, not from their relationships to things. The signified
might even be said to supplant or evacuate the referent. For Lacan,
the word brings about the "murder" of the thing.[21]

Since with the utterance of the word "I" the subject, too, expe-
riences a phenomenal "fading,"[22] to be thrown into language is,
once again, to be given over to death.[23] Indeed, Lacan himself suggests that it is more through the signifier than anything else that we
can experience our Being-towards-death.[24] At the point of the entry into language, the infant subject is confronted with a stark alternative: "being" or meaning.[25] She inevitably chooses meaning,
since without meaning there is no humanity. She suffers thence-
forth from a *manque-à-être*: from a lack of "being." Once again,
though, a certain limited freedom awaits the subject who is subsequently prepared to acknowledge that she is a "not" or a "nullity."

As every reader of Ferdinand de Saussure knows, the value of a
word is defined through two kinds of differences, one of which is

"paradigmatic," and the other "syntagmatic."[26] Paradigmatic relations are those linking one word to another at the level of the *langue* or system of a language. A word is defined through its difference from its synonyms, homonyms, and the words which constitute its "class" (e.g., in the case of the word *red*, the words *blue*, *yellow*, *green*, and *black*). Such relations are not immutable, but they are so stable as to seem given for all time. They define language in its "before me," "after me," and "always bigger than me" aspects.

However, a word's value is not only defined by its paradigmatic or systemic relations, but also by its syntagmatic or discursive ones—by the relations between it and the words which surround it in the concrete clause, sentence, and paragraph of which it is a part. Word combinations are never codified to the degree that paradigmatic relations are, since all of us have to be in a position to use the same word in multiple contexts. And while word order is always subject to certain rules, poets know that these rules exist as much to be meaningfully broken as slavishly adhered to. Syntagmatic relations can consequently reverse the paradigmatic expectations we have about a word, or extend the meaning of that word in new and surprising directions.

We also always exercise a certain amount of liberty at the level of word selection. We can choose one particular word from the many words to which it is paradigmatically related in order to communicate the particularity of what we want to say. Even more important in this respect are the semantic transformations which we are able to precipitate by aligning words from one paradigmatic group with words from another, whether by combining them with each other or by substituting them for each other.

But what I am calling "individuation" has only in part to do with such qualities as "voice," "style," "idiolect," and other linguistic markers that point toward what we typically think of as the speaking subject. Even more crucially, it has to do with how we symbolize the world. Although to deploy our significatory faculties on behalf of other beings is seemingly to direct them away from

ourselves as speakers to an external referent, it is in fact more constitutive than any other kind of speech of subjective singularity.
Every time we name a new creature or thing, we become more and
more unlike anyone else who ever lived. This symbolic capacity
is, however, only available to the subject who has submitted early
in life not just to *one* loss, but to *two* losses. We are no more ourselves responsible for the second of these losses than the first. It,
too, occurs only as the result of our insertion into a preexisting symbolic order.

In addition to connoting "linguistic organization," "history,"
and "a specific set of social and economic circumstances," the *da*
in every *Dasein* connotes "a kinship structure." As Lévi-Strauss
suggests, "kinship structure" is virtually synonymous with a particular incest taboo or set of incest taboos;[27] it means the impossibility of possessing a particular sexual object. We are conventionally
thrown into our designated kinship structure, which prohibits sexual intercourse between parents and children, through the Oedipus
complex.

Since two of the typical end results of the Oedipus complex are
the subject's assumption of a position within sexual difference and
the installation at the level of the unconscious either of the mother
or the father as the first love object, it is often assumed that the primary function of the Oedipus complex is social normalization. I
am no longer as certain as I once was that the Oedipus complex is
adequate to this task. It does, however, satisfy an irreducible *structural* imperative. This is not to facilitate exchange between families,
as Lévi-Strauss argues. It is, rather, to effect a psychic opening up.

In eroticizing a particular familial axis or set of axes, the Oedipus complex awakens something in us which none of us can do
without—the capacity to be concerned with someone besides ourselves. And, in obliging us to surrender the one we love for a series
of substitute love objects, it makes "room" in our psyche, and so in
the world, for other people and things. The loss of our first love-
object is always tragic, but it is the precondition for care. Only if
we pay this exorbitant price early in our lives can things and other

people "matter" to us. Indeed, the case could be stated even more starkly: only because we are thrown into a kinship structure can there *be* a world.

ʿDAS DINGʾ

The entry into language does not simply precipitate the "fading" of "being"; it also gives rise to an unsatisfiable urge to symbolize what we have lost. The *je ne sais quoi* which each of us thereafter lacks, and to which all of our acts of signification will never be adequate, represents less an object than a nonobject: the impossible nonobject of desire. In *Seminar VII*, Lacan designates this impossible nonobject of desire with one of German's numerous words for "thing": *das Ding*. He also stresses that it does not preexist its loss.[28]

The experience of being within the "here and now" is completely ineffable—it defies every kind of symbolization. Once presence evaporates, however, it assumes a status which it did not have before: it comes to signify a lost fullness.[29] This is because we are able to constitute something as an object of desire only when we are able to make it a representative of something anterior, something no longer available to us. As Jean-Joseph Goux suggests in his essay on numismatics, "Metaphors, symptoms signs, representations: it is always through replacement that values are created. Replacing what is forbidden, what is lacking, what is hidden or lost, what is damaged, in short, replacing with something equivalent what is not itself, in person, presentable."[30] The loss of "being" makes possible this substitutory transaction.

But desire entails more than simple retroaction; it also involves the "naming," as it were, of the "unnameable." Each new libidinal object not only derives its value through reference back to the originary nonobject, but also provides the latter with lineaments and a face, transforms the "nothing" into a "something." To desire is thus initially to incarnate, and later to reincarnate, the "what-has-been." The latter is an endlessly expanding category. Over time, it comes to consist of a complex and multifaceted constellation of signifiers, which provides both a record of all of the ways each of us has loved in the past, and an opening up of the new ways each of us will be able to love in the future.

In attributing the inception of desire to the loss of "being," rather than an originary love-object, Lacan seems to open the way toward something which many of us have long dreamed of: an a-Oedipal or even anti-Oedipal psychoanalysis. However, he himself shows no interest in moving in this direction. Over and over again in his seminars and writings, Lacan insists upon the twofoldedness of the entry into language. With what seems to be not merely a compulsive but also a compulsory repetitiveness, he tells us that the simple loss of "being" or the "here and now" is not by itself sufficient to set the wheels of desire in motion. The sacrifice must be repeated, the loss reexperienced. Therefore the Oedipus complex and the castration crisis must follow close upon the heels[31] of the "fading" or "aphanisis" of "being."[32]

The vehemence with which Lacan asserts and reasserts this point is clearly in part ideologically motivated. However, it is not merely out of the wish to maintain existing social relations that he so speaks. First, it would seem incontrovertibly the case that there can be no experience of loss until it has been represented through a second loss. None of us is really aware of choosing meaning rather than "being." Not only do we pass imperceptibly from the latter to the former, but we ourselves do not really exist until after that transition has been effected. Second, retroaction, which is the precondition for all psychic value, is missing until *das Ding* has been relinquished. It is therefore only with the metaphoric repetition of this originary loss that can we be said to lose anything of consequence.

Since *das Ding* is not so much an object as a nonobject, it is also insufficient by itself to connect us to the world of things. This crucial function is performed by whatever human or other being serves as our first real object. It is therefore with a classically parental signifier that libidinal symbolization begins, and through constant reference back to that signifier that it continues. In addition, it is only in our relationship to our first real object that each of us learns to love. Because it consists only of a clinging and presumably often suffocating presence, life in the "here and now" is inimical to love or any other real affective relation. Consequently, we could not be said to "love" and then to "lose" it. Rather, we lose "being" and only thereafter, with much difficulty, learn to love its representatives. The Oedipus complex is the crucial site of that ascesis.

Finally, as I will argue in Chapter 5, it is only with the loss of the originary love-object that *das Ding* definitively emerges as the impossible nonobject of desire. Prior to this second loss, the subject is not inside language. She also suffers from what might be called libidinal aphasia. Only with the relegation of the originary love-object to the unconscious is the *hic et nunc* evacuated from the psyche, and the subject brought within libidinal speech. The incest taboo provides the agency which secures this repression.

It might nevertheless seem a contradiction in terms to root the subject's highly particular signifying capacities in the loss of its original love-object. Have we not learned from psychoanalysis that there is precious little room here for psychic individuation—that those who love and lose their fathers choose men who resemble them as replacements, just as those who love and lose their mothers choose women who resemble their mothers? And do not the parental figures finally approximate something like symbolic constructs, whose importance radically exceeds the persons in question?

Although this view of the Oedipus complex prevails not only in antipsychoanalytic, but also in most psychoanalytic circles, Freud himself suggests otherwise. In "Mourning and Melancholia," he defines a love-object as a radically heterogeneous collocation of memories, to all of which we could never have simultaneous access, and the relative importance of which can presumably shift over time.[33] The process of mourning is lengthy, he tells us, because we must say good-bye to each of these memories in turn.

Surprisingly, rather than providing yet another impetus to conceptualize desire a-Oedipally, phenomenology encourages us to think in a similar way about the mother and father. There is nothing upon which Heidegger more passionately insists than upon the importance of deentifying the world we inhabit. "The Thing" is only one of the texts in which he attempts to teach us to stop thinking of it as a collocation of present-at-hand objects, and to allow it to emerge in its full and nontotalizable complexity. When we apprehend a jar in its true Being, he suggests in that text, it ceases to be a lowly vessel and becomes the dwelling place for earth and sky, humans and divinities.[34] And if even a seemingly insignificant jar can be as rich in value and meaning as Heidegger shows it to be, how much more must this be the case with those whom we love with the full force of our first-felt passion?

Heidegger has of course little to say about the implications for desire of his complex and expansive account of a thing. Psychoanalysis, however, teaches us how difficult it is to generalize about the libidinal history to which the conglomerate of parental memories gives rise. As Freud's analysis of dreams, jokes, and parapraxes makes clear, the displacements at the heart of psychic life are no more at the absolute behest of the larger culture than they are at the simple disposition of the conscious individual.[35] Because of the unstable and heterogeneous nature of every love-object, desire can extend itself in entirely unpredictable directions. Perhaps what permits an early love-object to replace the mother, for instance, is not the smell of breast milk, but the name "Persephone," which seems to the infant subject akin to the mother's name, "Penelope," and which leads, through many detours and circumlocutions, to an adult passion for classical literature. And for another subject, the word "mother" might signify a mole at the corner of a shapely mouth, which she many years later rediscovers on the face of an eighteen-year-old boy.

Our object-choices are also always made from within specific geographical, social, economic, and historical circumstances. These circumstances can profoundly inflect our unconscious signifying network and so further particularize it. We might think, in this respect, of the role played by the servant girl in Freud's case history of the Wolfman, whose posture while washing the floor establishes the erotic disposition of a middle-class man.[36] Equally germane to the present discussion is the geographical displacement implicit in the slippage from the English "glance" to the German *Glanz* in Freud's essay on fetishism; here, the movement from one language and culture to another determines a shine on the nose as the compensatory supplement.[37] Although most subjects make an initial libidinal investment either in their mother or their father, it is impossible to say in advance where any one of them will go from there.

LANGUAGE OF DESIRE

Although a kinship structure represents a *langue*, the libidinal acts with which we speak this *langue* do not constitute discrete and evanescent instances of *parole*, or speech. Rather, each one builds upon and at times transforms those which precede it, and anticipates and makes possible those which follow it. Each libidinal speech act also finds its signified in those which came before. This constantly expanding and mutating constellation of signifiers constitutes a language—the language of our desire. It is by glimpsing at least part of this constellation that we hear the call summoning us to ourselves. And it is by becoming passionate about its expansion that we assume our "there."

But when we speak our language of desire, we do more than individuate ourselves. We also render what we speak about more real, more true, more "itself." This is because libidinal signification has an *ontological* force. By allowing another being to embody *das Ding*, we bring it from the darkness of invisibility into the radiance of appearance. We therefore induct that creature or thing into its Being. This may seem an outrageous claim, and one to which neither Lacan nor Heidegger would accede. However, it is on the basis of Lacan's own explicit dialogue with a Heideggerian text that I advance it.

The Heidegger text to which I refer is "The Thing" ("Das Ding"). In this essay, Heidegger sets himself the task of clarifying what a thing "is," in the most profound sense of the word—what status it enjoys at the moment that it is allowed to stand forth "into the unconcealedness of what is already present" (168). He attempts to explain, that is, what a thing becomes at the moment that it appears. Heidegger effects this clarification in part by differentiating a thing from an object, and in part through an extended comparison of *Dasein* to a potter.

Unlike an object, Heidegger writes, a thing is not an entifying representation. It is not something which the human subject places upright in front of her, in implicit opposition to herself (167). Heidegger uses *das Ding* to refer to a thing. He designates an object with the compound word *Gegenstand. Gegenstand* brings together *gegen*, which means "against," with *der Stand*, which means "standing position."

However, if a thing is not something we produce, it is also not something pregiven, something which precedes the advent of *Dasein*. It is, rather, what emerges from a particular relationship between *Dasein* and the world, a relationship which is different in every respect from that which gives rise to an object. "Vigilance" is the name which Heidegger here gives to this relationship, but it could as well be "care." "When and in what way do things appear as things?" he asks. He then provides the following, carefully worded answer: "They do not appear *by means of* human making. But neither do they appear without the vigilance of mortals" (181).

After insisting that a thing is not the product of human activity, Heidegger suggests with seeming inconsistency that it is we who shape it. But this shaping has less to do with the outer form of the thing than with the emptiness it encompasses. Vigilant *Dasein* could be compared to a potter, and a thing to the jar she crafts. This metaphoric potter "does not, strictly speaking, make the jug." Rather, she sculpts the void in its form. As Heidegger puts it, "from start to finish the potter takes hold of the impalpable void and brings it forth as the container in the shape of a containing vessel" (169). It could even be said to be in the void rather than the clay that the jug's "thingness" inheres. In order to make this point more forcefully, Heidegger has metaphoric recourse to another of the exemplary jug's attributes: its capacity to contain what is put into it. He suggests that the potter might almost be said to "pour" the void into the jug (172), and thereby to make it a thing.

When attempting to clarify what makes vigilant *Dasein* resemble a potter, Heidegger reverts to a central concept from *Being and Time*: Being-towards-death. "Death is the shrine of Nothing, that is, of that which in every respect is never something that merely exists, but is rather something that presences at the same time as Being itself," he writes.[38] He thereby suggests that it is by virtue of our mortality that we have the capacity to become shapers of the void—that it is out of the nothingness toward which we are moving that we summon the essence of things. But mortality is something which must be *assumed*; it is not automatically a human attribute (179). It is consequently presumably only through Being-towards-death that we acquire the capacity to "be-thing."

In *Seminar VII*, Lacan engages in an extended dialogue with Heidegger's essay, transforming in the process the meaning of the void. In the passage in which he does so, he makes Heidegger's primary metaphor—the jar—his own, although he refers to it throughout as a vase. He thereby renders explicit his very unpsychoanalytic interest in "thingness." Lacan also maintains with Heidegger that it is through crafting an empty space in the form of the jar that we make it a thing; the section in which he makes his most explicit references to Heidegger is even entitled "On creation ex nihilo."[39]

However, Lacan refers to what results from our sculpting efforts not as *das Ding*, but rather as *die Sache*. Here, as elsewhere, he reserves the term *das Ding* for that term whose absence creates the void. Lacan thereby helps us to understand that to be-thing something is not simply to shape a nothingness; it is also to establish a relationship between this thing and another term. More precisely, it is to wrap the shape of this thing around the space created through the evacuation of the other term. "Now if you consider the vase from the point of view I first proposed," he writes in *Seminar VII*, as an object meant to represent the existence of the emptiness at the center of the real that is called [*das Ding*], this emptiness . . . presents itself as a *nihil*, as nothing. And that is why the potter, just like you to whom I am speaking, creates the vase with his hand around this emptiness, creates it, just like the mythical creator, *ex nihilo*, starting with a hole. (121)

The value which we confer on a thing when we sculpt the void in its image is extrinsic; it comes from elsewhere. It might seem, therefore, to be the kind of value a commodity has, a value which ultimately works to cheapen rather than enrich. However, Lacan remarks that when we mold our nothingness in the form of another creature or thing, we "raise" this creature or thing to the "dignity" of *das Ding* (118). He thereby helps us to understand that the value which we bestow is neither relative nor equivalent;[40] it is, rather, absolute. To allow another being to represent the impossible nonobject of desire is to grant it a worth beyond all possibility of reckoning: to make it the embodiment of something like the "all-in-all." And, since this all-in-all was never existentially available to any of us, but emerges as such only through the evacuation of presence, there is no way of returning to it. The act of symbolization can be repeated in another form, but not reversed.

It is not only by gesturing toward what I am calling "absolute value," a concept which would be anathema to Heidegger himself,[41] that Lacan complicates the phenomenological account of "thingness"; Lacan also does not hesitate to equate *die Sache* with an object. Indeed, *die Sache* signifies for Lacan the object par excellence—the object of desire. He thereby gives voice to what Heidegger cannot finally bring himself to say. The void—or, as Heidegger will elsewhere call it, the "clearing"[42]—has a psychic consistency. It is produced through the evacuation of spatial and temporal presence, and is kept open only through the continued operation of desire.

AN ETHICS OF DESIRE

Near the end of *Seminar VII*, Lacan elaborates an ethics which runs counter to everything that has ever been written about the moral life. He advances the claim that it is through the practice of desire rather than through its renunciation that humans approach what has traditionally been called virtue. "The only thing of which one can [finally] be guilty is of having given ground relative to one's desire," he repeats over and over (319, 321, and 322).

This would seem to be an ethics which only a Lacanian would propose. Astonishingly, however, Heidegger, too, emphasizes the intimate conjunction of the erotic and the ethical in "The Thing." In the passage in which he does so, he unabashedly celebrates love's ontological benefits. He does so through an exploration of the etymological connection between the Roman word *realitas* and human "concern"; what is important to us, he demonstrates, becomes more real (175–76). Heidegger also suggests that love's benefits flow in two directions. We enrich not merely the world, but also ourselves when we care: "Love is of such a nature that it changes man into the things he loves," he says, in an approving paraphrase of a sentence from Meister Eckhart (176). Finally, as we have seen, Heidegger also links the concept of guilt to the failure to care. If we are for Heidegger unavoidably rather than avoidably guilty, it is in a sense because we can never care enough.

Later in the same essay, Heidegger explains that the relationship between *Dasein* and the jar, which vigilance makes possible, gives rise to a special kind of "mirroring." This mirroring is based not on likeness, but on a "simple belonging to one another" of human and thing which sets each "free into its own"—upon an "enfolding clasp" which "binds" each into "freedom" (179). In inducting the jar into its Being, it seems, we ourselves enter Being. As if to make this point as concretely as possible, Heidegger reminds us that such a receptacle has the capacity not only to contain liquids, but also to pour them—not only to receive them, but also to give them. For this reason, we who conjure things out of the void are at the same time "be-thinged" (181).

Lacan makes a similar argument in *Seminar VII*, although less directly. In attempting to clarify why we must not give ground relative to our desire, he has recourse to a peculiar metaphor. Our desire is a "destiny," he maintains, but a destiny which consists less of an advance than a return. We are guilty if we attempt to break with this destiny, because it is a debt which must be paid: it is our obligation to go back, again and again, to that good which is our particular good. "If analysis has a meaning," he explains, "desire is nothing other than that which supports an unconscious theme, the very articulation of that which roots us in a particular destiny, and that destiny demands insistently that the debt be paid, and desire keeps coming back, keeps returning, and situates us once again in a given track, the track of something that is specifically our business" (319).

The cross-references linking *Seminar VII* to "The Thing" are in this case even more explanatory of the first of those texts than of the second. Through them, we are able to understand that what Lacan calls "our business" is also the world's business. To say that "desire keeps coming back, keeps returning, and situates us in a given track" is to say that each of us enjoys the capacity to raise particular *Sachen* to the status of *das Ding*—to bring certain creatures and certain things into the brilliance of a more-than-reality. To each of us, through our particular libidinal history, has been given the potentiality for participating in a unique series of disclosures. This potentiality is not so much a talent as a responsibility. When we fail to realize it, we are bottomlessly guilty.

Metaphors proliferate as Lacan attempts to elaborate what it means to remain on the path of our desire. It entails remaining "a long way from our *jouissance*" (185); not merely paying the pound of flesh or "being," but also affirming the sacrifice. It means "incorporat[ing] the signifier" (294). Finally, it implies "eating the book" (322). With this last metaphor, we are again recognizably in theological territory, and Lacan himself acknowledges as much. The trope comes from Revelations,[43] a text devoted to the end of time. Here, however, Revelations and Genesis coincide.

To eat the book means to embrace signification, and thereby not merely to experience but also to affirm the eclipse of "being." This eclipse of "being" is itself the condition for something much

more important—for Being, or what Lacan calls the "properly apoc-
alyptic creation" (294). And once again, this sublation from "being" to Being is something which befalls the creator as fully as it
does the metaphoric jar or world. The creator becomes what she
creates.

Lacan is very precise about the terms of this transformation,
which he elaborates in the form of an autobiographical parable:
"When I ate the book, I didn't thereby become the book, any more
than the book became flesh," he explains. "The book became *me* so
to speak" (322). The difference between the first of these possibilities and the last may seem infinitesimal, but it is in fact vast. It is
the difference between a simple self-expropriation and what Heidegger would call an "expropriative appropriati[on]";[44] between the
dispiriting apprehension of the otherness of one's self, and the ecstatic rediscovery, at the site of the other, of one's utmost "ownness."

THE PASSION OF THE SIGNIFIER

In acceding to the incest taboo, every subject finds herself
obliged to search in the future for the past. However, not every subject embraces this imperative. The loss of the originary love-object
generally gives rise to one of two contrary libidinal impulses: an insistence upon the return which every displacement might be said to
stage, or a valorization of each new term in its particularity. In the
first of these cases, desire focuses exclusively upon the similarity
which links the substitute to the term which precedes it, discard-
ing everything about the substitute which is in excess of its representative function. In the second, it savors that within the replacement term which distinguishes it from all previous thematizations
of the original nonobject, placing the premium on the surplus or
supplement.

The subject who is under the sway of the second of these impulses remains outside the temporality of desire, rooted in the present. Apprehending only the "new" and the "different" in each new
love-object, she fails to see that what she now cares about represents

the reincarnation of what she has previously cared about. She consequently discloses other beings without realizing that she is doing so, confusing appearance with substance. The subject who seeks obsessively to return to the past also remains exterior to the temporality of desire, and fails to understand that passion is a semiotic affair. This subject, however, does not simply disclose other creatures and things blindly; she refuses disclosure altogether. For her, everything that exists has value only as a memorial for what was. Consequently, rather than reembodying the past, she disembodies the present.

As should be clear by now, neither where the compulsive urge to return nor where the single-minded valorization of uniqueness prevails could we be said to eat the book. The expropriative appropriation about which both Heidegger and Lacan speak can occur only when we not only signify our passion, but are also passionate about the libidinal signifier. To be passionate about the libidinal signifier means to know that one's capacity to care is rooted in the past, but that—until the moment of death—it will always be subject to retroactive rearticulations. It also means to love and cherish the precise forms in which the impossible nonobject of desire can be miraculously reborn. Finally, to be passionate about the libidinal signifier means to cultivate the rhetorician's enthusiasm for fresh metaphors and metonymies. It is never to tire of crafting the void within one into new shapes, new patterns, and new colors.

3

LISTENING TO LANGUAGE

Unlike our linguistic speech acts, our libidinal ones remain for the most part unconscious. Not only do we usually not know what we are saying; we do not even know that we are in the constant process of making signifiers out of the phenomenal world. Even when the common wheat field which we have passed every day of our eighteenth summer without noticing it suddenly assumes the radiance of a Van Gogh painting, we are unlikely to attribute the transformation to an act of libidinal signification. This is because our ignorance of the signifiers through which we care is not based upon simple indifference; rather, repression blocks our access to them. Although representing what is most emphatically our own, the language of our desire consequently remains for most of us irreducibly Other. In a certain sense, we do not even speak it; rather, it speaks us.

How, then, could any of us ever arrive at that state of exultant symbolization which I described in the previous chapter? How could any subject in the world ever "eat" the book of his desire? And what justifies me in referring to the constellation of signifiers through which we care as a "language"? The primary function of a word is communication; like a coin passed from one hand to another,[1] it links the members of a *socius* to each other. If our libidinal speech-acts are opaque even to us, how can we expect others to understand them?

Surprising as it may sound, the constellation of signifiers through which we care can be translated into a communicable form. And when we exteriorize our language of desire in the form of an address to other subjects, it also becomes intelligible to us. We thus find ourselves in a position to do something we could not otherwise do: to claim our disclosive powers. We do so not by taking possession[2] of them, but only through those self-expropriating appropriations about which both Heidegger and Lacan speak.

Although I have invoked the authors of "Das Ding" and *Seminar VII* in making this last assertion, the argument I will be advancing here exceeds the mandate of both texts in a number of ways. This is, however, only an apparent contradiction. Only by putting Heidegger and Lacan once again in dialogue with each other will we find the theoretical coordinates for conceptualizing that process whereby we "own" the self of care. This time, however, the conversation will take place between not two interlocutors, but rather three: between Lacan, the Heidegger of *Being and Time*, and the Heidegger of such later texts as *Parmenides* and *On the Way to Language*.

THE HOUSE OF BEING

Although based on a 1935 seminar, Heidegger's *An Introduction to Metaphysics* contains two sentences which could serve as an epigraph to *Being and Time* (1927): "In accordance with the hidden message of the beginning, man should be understood, within the question of being, as *the* site which being requires in order to disclose itself. Man is the site of the openness, the there."[3] For the Heidegger of *Being and Time* disclosure is a definitionally *human* act; *Dasein* and only *Dasein* can provide the clearing within which Being appears. Not merely does this role belong to man alone; it is also man who determines whether or not he will attend to Being in this way. He does so by being either "resolute" or "irresolute" in relation to his heritage.

These were not claims that Heidegger was prepared to stand by. In his subsequent retreat from all forms of willing, he became increasingly suspicious of human agency. He also became more and more skeptical about all forms of humanism, with their prioritization of man. In Heidegger's later writings, resoluteness consequently gives way to "letting be" as the exemplary manifestation of *Dasein*,[4] and another space must be found for the disclosure of Being. Heidegger finds that disclosive space in language. In his "Letter on Humanism" (1947), he maintains that it is not *Dasein*, but rather language, which provides the "house of Being."[5] We are at most only the residents and guardians of this house, and often far less.

In "Letter on Humanism," Heidegger still insists upon the intimate connection between man and language. The word is not merely the "house of Being," but also the "home" of *Dasein* (217). However, in "The Nature of Language" (1959), Heidegger at times emphasizes the disjunctive relation between language and *Dasein*. Language "always is ahead of us," he writes, always in excess of our capacity to speak it.[6] And, far from "using" language, it might be said to "use" us, even to "master" us. We can only "endure it," "suffer it," "receive it as it strikes us and submit to it" (57). In ". . . Poetically Man Dwells . . ." (1954), Heidegger even goes so far as to detach language altogether from *Dasein*, to make it both speaker and spoken. "Strictly, it is language that speaks," he writes in the same text. "Man first speaks when, and only when, he responds to language by listening to its appeal."[7]

Nevertheless, even in those texts in which Heidegger seems most insistent upon the primacy and autonomy of language in bringing about the disclosure of Being, he cannot help but acknowledge the impossibility of conceptualizing it in absolute isolation from *Dasein*. "Man is . . . needful to language, that he may speak it," writes Heidegger in "The Nature of Language" (90). Elsewhere in the same text, he indicates that it is only from "Saying" that "it comes to pass that the World is [allowed] to appear"; therefore, the human mouth could be said to represent the flower bed in which the word blossoms (101).

There is also a certain ambiguity in "Letter on Humanism" about where the clearing is to be found. Although in one of the most important passages from that text we learn that language is the site of Being's disclosure (230), on the preceding page Heidegger acknowledges that he attributes that role to *Dasein* in *Being and Time* (229). He also spends much of the rest of the essay trying to reconcile these two contrary claims. Ultimately, Heidegger maintains that man does indeed represent the clearing, but only insofar as he is "ek-sistent," outside himself in language (252). And "in this nearness, in the clearing of the *Da*, man dwells as the ek-sisting one without yet being able properly to experience and take over this dwelling" (241). It seems that, although language is the "house of Being," it can assume this function only when properly tended by its human guardian.

Heidegger also personalizes language on more than one occasion in his later writings. In *Parmenides*, a text based upon a 1942–43 lecture series, he suggests that "the poetry of a poet or the treatise of a thinker stands within its own proper unique word."[8] By defining the disclosive word as an idiosyncratic word, he links it ineluctably to a particular speaker. Heidegger thus renders null and void the distinction that he makes elsewhere between language and *Dasein*. It is difficult not to place considerable emphasis upon this sentence, given Heidegger's continued hostility to standardized language and all other manifestations of the "they." And in a subsequent work, "The Way to Language" (1959), Heidegger suggests once again, and even more forcefully, that language comes into its own only when it is spoken in a highly individualized way: "We can give a name to the appropriation that prevails in Saying: it—Appropriation—appropriates or owns. When we say this, we speak our own appropriate already spoken language."[9]

"Appropriate" here means not only a word which is fitting to what is named, but also one which is specific to, or owned by, a particular speaker.[10] Heidegger's use of the word in this double sense attests to the impossibility of separating a disclosive utterance from the one who speaks it. The only disclosive or appropriate word is one which is owned or appropriated. This is because such a word is not so much a concept or a sound as a "relation": a relation between speaker and world. That relation is affective and its name is "care."

Surprisingly, in "Letter on Humanism," the very text in which he turns away from *Dasein* to language as the "house of Being," Heidegger offers perhaps his most explicit and passionate account of the affective bases of disclosure: "To embrace a 'thing' or a 'person' in its essence means to love it, to favor it. Thought in a more original way such favoring [*Mögen*] means to bestow essence as a gift. Such favoring is the proper essence of enabling, which not only can achieve this or that but also can let something essentially unfold in its provenance, that is, let it be" (220). In this extraordinary passage, Heidegger asks us to think the following paradox, which is resistant to all rationalizing gestures: it is only by embracing other people and things that we can free them to be themselves—only by enfolding them within our psychic enclosure that we can create the space where they can emerge from concealment.

What is true for others is of course also true for us: our Being, too, is a gift from elsewhere. Most of us do not relish the thought that our value has been conjured out of some other person's void. We wish to believe that our beauty is strictly our own. It is perhaps the most difficult of all lessons to learn that it is our essence not only to appropriate, in the Heideggerian rather than the Cartesian sense of that word, but also to be so appropriated.

A PRESENCE MADE OF ABSENCE

By elaborating the semiotic bases of affect—by showing that there is no language without desire, and no desire which is not itself language—Lacan provides the basis for thinking the Heidegger of *Being and Time* together with the Heidegger of the "Letter on Humanism." But the case must be stated even more forcefully: Lacan shows us the *necessity* of thinking these two Heideggers together. The clearing is neither language nor *Dasein*, but rather the psychic void opened up in *Dasein* by language. We allow the world to appear, and so to Be, by making it a signifier of what has been lost to us through the advent of meaning.

Lacan says of the word that it "murders" the thing.[11] Heidegger, on the other hand, maintains that "the word . . . gives Being to the thing."[12] It might therefore seem difficult to reconcile Lacan's theory of language with Heidegger's in the way I propose doing. However, in "Function and Field of Speech and Language in Psychoanalysis," the same text in which he comments upon the murderous qualities of language, Lacan offers a formulation which is virtually identical to Heidegger's. "It is the world of words that creates the world of things," he writes (65). Lacan thereby makes evident that what he calls "murder" and what he calls "creation" are two sides of the same process.

In obliging us to conceptualize these two seemingly antagonistic terms together, Lacan is in effect reiterating and enlarging upon one of Heidegger's central points: in order for a thing to appear, or emerge as such, it must be "thinged."[13] To "thing" something is to make it "present." But this particular presence is affective, not temporal or spatial; affective presence requires, in fact, the *loss* of the "here and now." A thing is thus "a presence made of absence."[14] Lacan clarifies this point in a passage from the Rome discourse in which he discusses the *fort/da* game recounted by Freud in *Beyond the Pleasure Principle*:[15]

Through the word—already a presence made of absence—absence gives itself a name in that moment whose perpetual recreation Freud's genius detected in the play of the child. And from this pair of sounds modulated . . . there is born the world of meaning of a particular language in which the world of things will come to be arranged. (65)

A thing must be extracted from the *hic et nunc* in order to appear because appearance is a temporal event. Only by being alienated from itself, and caught up in a complex process of retroaction and anticipation, can a thing come into its Being. The gift from the word to the thing is thus time, as Lacan suggests in *Seminar I*.[16] Now we understand why Heidegger's later account of language cannot be thought apart from his earlier account of *Dasein*. Since temporality is a strictly human category, this gift can only be conferred by *Dasein*. If the word can be the "*time of the thing*" (Lacan's emphasis), that is because *Dasein* has paid the price for there to be a past and future.

The passage I quoted a moment ago attributes the gift of Being not to language per se, but to a "particular language." Any utterance, it seems, can bring about the annihilation of the "here and now," but only a highly personalized one can make it live again in a new way. The words "particular language" represent Sheridan's addition; Lacan himself writes *langue*. However, Lacan advances a similar claim to Sheridan's in *Seminar VII*,[17] in his discussion of sublimation. In this text, Lacan insists upon the libidinal determinants behind all creative acts of symbolization. At least from the retrospective vantage point of that later text, the brief discussion of the world-making capacities of the signifier which Lacan offers in "Function and Field of Speech and Language in Psychoanalysis" can consequently be seen as a meditation upon what Heidegger calls "appropriation"—upon that very singular word which functions simultaneously to disclose speaker and what is spoken about. For the psychoanalyst, as for the phenomenologist, language "presences" only when it is "owned."

In spite of the many affinities which can now be seen to link Lacan's account of language with Heidegger's, there would still seem to be one insuperable obstacle in the way of reading them together in the way I am proposing, and that is Heidegger's refusal to conceptualize within the parameters of the sign. In Heidegger's view, words do not point to other words; rather, they disclose Being.

Language does not *signify*; rather, it *shows*. Lacan, on the other hand, frequently evokes both Saussure and Lévi-Strauss in the *Écrits*, and always in a spirit of appreciation.[18]

However, to imagine that Heidegger's repudiation of the concept of signification puts him at odds with Lacan is to overlook the complex transformation to which the latter subjects the same concept. First of all, Lacan dismantles Saussure's concept of the linguistic sign. For him, there can be no fixed relation of linguistic signifier and signified, but only a "sliding" of the signified under the signifier.[19] Words can consequently not be imprisoned within the function to which Saussure would relegate them, the function of the sign.

Second, Lacan strips words of the primacy which Saussure confers upon them. At least within the account of signification which he offers in *Seminar VII*, the perceptual signifier precedes the verbal, and provides it with its signified. It is also by looking rather than by speaking that we utter our language of desire—through the image rather than the word that we raise objects (*die Sachen*) to the status of the impossible nonobject of desire (*das Ding*).

Lacan begins *Seminar VII* with an extensive discussion of Freud's *Project for a Scientific Psychology*,[20] a text which is centrally concerned with the elaboration of the predominantly visual *Bahnung*, the unconscious signifying chain.[21] In this discussion, moreover, he too insists that it is by means of *Wahrnehmungszeichen* or "signs of perception," that the unconscious speaks (65). Almost all of the examples of perceptual signifiers which he provides, moreover, are visual in nature: a collection of match boxes (114); the surprisingly good painting produced by a patient (116–17); the hats and dresses created by fashion designers (99); Heidegger's jar (119–21); macaroni noodles (121); and the intact beauty of Sade's Justine (202). Finally, Lacan stresses the importance, for the real, of our acts of perceptual signification.

The most important of Lacan's visual signifiers in this last respect is a Cézanne still-life painting. In the passage in which he discusses this painting, he attributes to Cézanne's painted apples the power to enhance or ennoble their worldly referent. "Everyone knows that there is a mystery in the way Cézanne paints apples," he observes, "for the relationship to the real as it is renewed in art at that moment makes the object appear purified; it involves a renewal of its dignity" (141). Lacan thereby deconstructs the age-old opposition of Being and seeming, and representation and the real. He suggests that, far from being either a despised copy of the natural fruit or their triumphant sublation into the superior domain of the aesthetic construction, these apples provide the means by which their living counterpart can become more truly itself.

With this account of Cézanne's apples, Lacan also helps us to understand why he imputes to the signifier the capacity not only to kill, but also to create. With the linguistic signifier, it seems, we cannot help but induce the "fading" of "being," render creatures and things absent. With the perceptual signifier, however, we can render these same creatures and things affectively present; we can bring them out the darkness of nonbeing and into the light of Being. The creative "word" is thus in fact an image.

But I do not mean to suggest that the perceptual signifier represents the simple antithesis of the linguistic. Although our language of desire is predominantly a visual language, it is classically by means of words that we make this language our own. This means in part that it is through translating what we see into speech that we generally assume it. But it also means that language can point the way to a different kind of vision: that it can be the agency whereby the look becomes "itself."

THE FUTURAL PAST

The Heidegger of *Being and Time* is as concerned with the past as he is with the future. Indeed, he emphasizes from the very beginning of this 1927 text that *Dasein* "*is* its past, whether explicitly or not" (41). This is not merely because thrownness, fully as much as mortality, defines us, but also because there is something in the past which—due to its repetitive force—might be said to be our future. Heidegger never clarifies precisely what he means by this chiasmus of past and future, but he maintains that it is primarily disclosed to us through our moods or states of mind (173).

Anxiety is the mood which most interests Heidegger. He suggests that anxiety arises when the subject is wrenched out of the "at-home" sentiment which predominates when he is absorbed in the "they" and brought "face to face with itself as a Being-in-the-world" (233). It is a sentiment which makes it possible for us to become conscious of our finitude—to understand that we are not "at home" in the world, are not in control of our ground. Although Heidegger does not have much to say about other particular moods, he repeatedly links the fact that we have them to our relation to other people and things—to our Being-with, and our Being-alongside. To be more precise, he suggests that they are indicative of our capacity to be concerned with the world. "*Essentially, a state-of-mind implies a disclosive submission to the world*," he writes, "*out of which we can encounter something that matters to us*" (177; Heidegger's emphasis).

Heidegger maintains that moods "temporaliz[e]" primarily in terms of "*having been*"; they bring us "*back to* something" (390; his emphasis). He even goes so far as to equate *Dasein*'s "thereness" with this "having been." However, this past comes to us from the future; it lies ahead of us instead of behind us. "The character of 'having been' arises from the future," Heidegger writes, and in such a way that the future which 'has been' . . . releases from itself the present. This phenomenon has the unity of a future which makes present in the process of having been" (374).

It is precisely by bringing us back to what was via what now approaches us that the futural past makes it possible for us to care about other creatures and things. This aspect of Heideggerian temporality consequently almost demands to be conceptualized in terms of that ever expanding constellation of affectively charged representations which constitutes each subject's language of desire, each term of which refers back to and derives its value from what came before.

But *Being and Time* does more than provide an important companion text to Lacan's *Seminar VII*; it also permits us to extend the latter in important ways. In that text, Heidegger distinguishes between two different ways of repeating the past, one of which he associates with inauthentic *Dasein*, and the other of which he associates with authentic *Dasein*. Normally, he suggests, we are so absorbed in collective thinking that we do not understand that our future is under the mandate of the past. We are therefore entirely in thrall to the what-has-been. We repeat it both blindly and passively. However, another kind of repetition is available to us, one which is both conscious and active. Rather than seeking to escape the past, we can "reverently preserve" it by welcoming its future manifestations (448–49).

Significantly, this repetition is not a mastery: it does not abolish the past, or even diminish its hold upon the future. Rather, it entails the recognition of what was and the acceptance of what must be. In other words, the subject once again freely chooses what he cannot avoid. Even more, he welcomes the recurrence of the past in the future as his ownmost possibility. "When historicality is authentic," Heidegger writes, "it understands history as the 'recurrence' of the possible, and knows that a possibility will recur only if existence is open for it fatefully, in a moment of vision, in resolute repetition" (444).

"Resoluteness," Heidegger's name for the psychic state through which we assume our past, usually signifies something like "determination" or "will." There is no question that it carries these meanings in *Being and Time* as well. However, in an important paragraph in "The Origin of the Work of Art," Heidegger offers a revisionary reading of that word. He suggests that "resoluteness" places *Dasein* in an "outstanding" relation to Being, rather than to itself. When we are resolute in the Heideggerian sense of the word, we do not reach beyond ourselves psychically in order to make some good our own. Instead, we extend ourselves welcomingly toward the world. "The resoluteness intended in *Being and Time* is not the deliberate action of a subject," writes Heidegger, "but the opening up of human being, out of its captivity in that which is, to the openness of Being."[22]

We open ourselves to the world when we embrace our futural past because it is via the world's visual forms that the past returns to us. Although this is seemingly a very un-Heideggerian claim, it is partially inspired by the metaphor with which Heidegger characterizes our resolute encounter with the what-has-been: "moment of vision." It is also in the spirit if not the letter of *Being and Time* that I say the following: to care about the world is actively to promote the conditions under which it can appear. Consequently, the subject who has assumed a Being-towards-death, and is therefore concerned about the being of others, does not seek to bury, forget, or transcend the past. Rather, this subject holds himself always open to new possibilities for the deployment of that signifying constellation which most profoundly individualizes him. He is receptive to the resurfacing in the present and future of what has been—not as an exercise in narcissistic solipsism, but rather as the extension in ever new directions of his capacity to care.

FREEDOM THROUGH REPETITION

What I have just described is once again something like an ethics of desire—an ethics grounded in a passion for symbolization, in a delight in the manifold and ever new forms that the past can assume. But it is not easy to account psychoanalytically for such a joyful, liberating, and discursive notion of return. For the most part, psychic repetition entails subjection rather than agency, and submersion in an apparent real, rather than access to the semiotic. And conscious resolve does not by itself seem a powerful enough force to reverse this situation.

As Freud makes clear both in *Beyond the Pleasure Principle* and his essay on "The Uncanny," we generally *compulsively* repeat the past. Freud cites as examples of this compulsive repetition the involuntary recollections by soldiers of traumatic events;[23] his own repeated return to the red-light district of a provincial Italian town during an afternoon walk, despite his conscious efforts to avoid going there;[24] and the story of a woman who married one man after another whom she must nurse to a premature death.[25] Each of these sufferers from compulsive repetition was astonished by the regularity with which he encountered, once again, what had been presumably left behind. Rather than recognizing this repetition as the "insistence" of a signifier specific to his own unconscious, each of these victims of compulsive repetition also responded to it as something coming from outside. For the most part, we, too, are ignorant of the signifiers which constitute our psychic "there," and react to the events by means of which they return to haunt us if their motivation were entirely external.

This is of course not the only kind of repetition discussed by Freud in *Beyond the Pleasure Principle*.[26] He accounts there both for the famous *fort/da* game and for the therapeutic cure as the domestication of a trauma by "speaking" it. By putting our memories into words, he maintains, it is possible to "bind" their affect and diminish their immediacy. In this way, we can shift from a passive to an active relation to the past; we can, indeed, "master" the what-has-been.[27] However, this second kind of repetition, based as it is on the desire for control and the depreciation of affect, is finally no closer to the kind of repetition I am attempting to theorize here than is the first.

Lacan maintains in "The Freudian Thing" that his project represents in a very strict sense a return to Freud.[28] However, in a vivid dramatization of the principle that a return often constitutes more than a simple replication, he elsewhere provides what Freud himself does not: a rich psychoanalytic account of how we might go about assuming the past. This account has the additional virtue of being both deeply informed by a reading of *Being and Time* and insistently focused upon the signifier. In "Function and Field of Speech and Psychoanalysis," Lacan describes the therapeutic situation as one within which the patient does not so much subjugate as claim the past. He claims the past by making it pass into the *verbe* or word. However, not just any word will do. For this purpose, the analysand must use "full" rather than "empty" speech.

That Lacan assigns a very different role to the analysand's language than does Freud is not likely to be apparent on a first reading of "Function and Field of Speech and Language in Psychoanalysis." The passage in that essay in which he most fully dramatizes the coming of the analysand to full speech appears at first glance disappointingly conventional. In full speech, Lacan writes, the analysand "brings back into present time the origins of his own person."

[H]e does this in a language that allows his discourse to be understood by his contemporaries, and which furthermore presupposes their present discourse. Thus it happens that the recitation of the *epos* may include a discourse of earlier days in its own archaic, even foreign language, or may even pursue its course in present time with all the animation of the actor; but it is like an indirect discourse, isolated in quotation marks within the thread of the narration, and, if the discourse is played out, it is on a stage implying the presence not only of the chorus, but also of spectators. (47)

This passage seems to do little more than restate the importance, within the therapeutic context, of "quoting" rather than "reliving" the past. Since through this affectively and existentially detached repetition the analysand is transformed from someone who is passively spoken by his desire to someone who actively speaks it, it seems to be the agency not only for "binding," but also for mastering the past.

However, this passage will prove upon closer scrutiny to underscore not *Dasein*'s mastery of the past, but rather its dependence upon the Other. It will also provide the impetus to conceptualize theater, not according to the model of Brechtian distantiation, but rather as a primarily affective event. This is, moreover, not the only passage in "Function and Field of Speech and Language in Psychoanalysis" to call into question man's sovereignty. In the most frequently cited paragraph from this text, Lacan offers his own version of what Heidegger would call "*Dasein*'s thrownness." Indeed, he provides an even bleaker account of the many ways in which our future might be said to be determined by the past than does the philosopher. And, although Lacan gives more agency to the letter than to facticity in defining who we are, he does so with the very Heideggerian end of establishing that we can never be in control of our ground:

> Symbols . . . envelop the life of man in a network so total that they join together, before he comes into the world, those who are going to engender him 'by flesh and blood'; so total that they bring to his birth, along with the gifts of the stars, if not with the gifts of fairies, the shape of his destiny; so total that they give the words that will make him faithful or renegade, the law of the acts that will follow him right to the very place where he *is* not yet and even beyond his death; and so total that through them his end finds its meaning in the last judgement, where the Word absolves his being or condemns it. (68)

Only one thing can mitigate this absolute predetermination, Lacan tells us at the end of this complex sentence: being "for" or "towards" death.

Lacan not only remains true here and elsewhere in the Rome discourse to the ethos of *Being and Time*; he goes one step further. He eliminates from the model he borrows from Heidegger the one concept which might seem to promise something like traditional agency: resolve. Lacan suggests that it is not through conscious will or determination that we orient ourselves toward our end, but rather through full speech. Within "Function and Field of Speech and Language in Psychoanalysis," Being-towards-death thus becomes a discursive effect. And, far from representing linguistic repetition as a vehicle for mastering the past, Lacan celebrates it there for its capacity to bring us up against the limits which define us.

Empty speech, which Lacan consistently defines in opposition to full speech, is the deployment of language on the part of the analysand to say "what" he is. It is predicated upon the belief that we can be spatially and temporally present to ourselves, and that language is a tool for effecting this self-possession. But instead of leading to self-possession, empty speech is the agency of an "evergrowing dispossession" (42). When we speak empty speech, we lift ourselves out of time, and freeze ourselves into an object or "statue" (43). We thereby undo ourselves as subjects.

Empty speech represents a refusal of symbolization in a second sense as well. It is what the analysand literally or metaphorically utters when he responds to the figural forms through which the past returns as if their value and meaning were immanent within them. Here, too, the analysand attempts to "entify" or "fill up" the signifier—to make it identical with itself. He refuses to accede to temporality, to the fact that every psychically important event depends for its value and meaning upon reference to an earlier or a later one. The analysand also fails to see that with his object-choices and other libidinal acts he is speaking a language of desire. Empty speech is what the analysand classically utters during the early stages of the analysis.

The later stages of the analysis ideally bring the subject to full speech. The analysand engages in full speech when he understands that his literal and metaphoric words are in fact signifiers—neither equivalent to things, nor capable of saying "what" they are, but rather a retroaction to and anticipation of other signifiers. Full speech is also speech in which the analysand recognizes within what he has previously taken to be the "here and now" the operations of a very personal system of signification—the operations, that is, of what Lacan calls his "*primary language*" (81; Lacan's emphasis).

To understand that one is the speaker of a particular language of desire is to know that the past cannot help but repeat itself in what will be. It is also to know that one's previous libidinal choices insist in the very words one utters. To grasp oneself as the speaker of a particular language of desire is consequently to apprehend the futural nature of the past, and to "reorder past contingencies by conferring on them the sense of necessities to come" (48).

But to assume one's language of desire implies more than apprehending the futural nature of the past. It also means accepting the condition upon which any of us speaks: *manque-à-être*. It means accepting, that is, we are beings who lack "being." This is only in part because of the "murderous" effect of words. It is also because what subjectivity finally represents is something like a "long speech."[29] And, as with the individual sentence, the meaning of this speech will be decided only with the final punctuation mark.

As Lacan puts it in "The Agency of the Letter in the Unconscious," "the signifier, by its very nature, always anticipates meaning by unfolding its dimension before it." Consequently, "as is seen at the level of the sentence when it is interrupted before the significant term: 'I shall never . . .', 'All the same it is . . .', 'And yet there may be . . .'" (153), we are in a constant relation of waiting with respect to meaning. We are waiting for meaning not only when we listen to someone else speak, but also with our own actions and object-choices. Since the word which will retroactively confer meaning upon the whole of our discourse and so determine who we will have been will only be uttered at the moment of death, to assume one's language of desire is to understand that event as the "'possibility which is one's ownmost, unconditional, unsupersedable, certain and as such indeterminable.'"[30] It is consequently to become "for" or "towards" death.

Although the assumption of our language of desire brings us up against our limits, it nevertheless represents the closest any of us will ever come to freedom. The one who begins actively speaking this language comes to understand that the past is not yet fully written—that "what is realized in [his] history is not the past definite of what was, since it is no more, or even the present perfect of what has been in what [is], but the future anterior of what [he] shall have been for what [he is]."[31] He is thereby released from the paralysis of being into the mobility of becoming.

LETTING LANGUAGE SAY ITS SAYING TO US

Because the Lacanian analysand comes to full speech only through the enactment and subsequent working through of the transference, the linguistic repetition whereby he assumes the past requires the presence of the analyst. During the transference, the analyst is physically present but metaphorically absent; he represents a figure or a group of figures from the analysand's previous life, and thereby makes available to scrutiny what would otherwise be concealed through repression. During the working through of the transference, the analysand eventually apprehends his relation to the analyst not as a contemporary reality, but rather as a repetition of a prior relation.[32] The analyst is then present primarily as a listener. In the first respect, Lacan's definition of the transference is faithful to Freud's. In the last respect, however, it differs significantly.

In the Freudian account, to work through the transference means to arrive at an understanding of the extraneousness of the analyst to the symbolic role he has been called upon to play. The analyst should consequently be present at the end of the analysis as himself—as what can no longer be assimilated to the past.[33] For Lacan, on the other hand, the analyst facilitates the cure by simple virtue of occupying the structural position of "listener." The analysand works through the transference by coming to understand that the analyst occupies this position, and by speaking accordingly.

This is only in part because to address one's words to another is to grasp the essentially dialogical nature of all speech. It is also because it is only in addressing our real or libidinal speech to an other that we can "hear" what we are saying. When we engage in a genuine dialogue with another, our words return to us from that other in a transformed guise. They come back to us derealized, as signifiers.[34] In *Seminar I*, Lacan consequently characterizes the analytic exchange as a "revolving dialogue":

Everything which is proffered from . . . the side of the subject, makes itself heard in B, on the side of the analyst.

The analyst hears it, but, in return, so does the subject. The echo of his discourse is symmetrical to the specularity of the image. This revolving dialogue . . . must finally bring [the subject] to [his unconscious self]. (283–84)

Heidegger also urges us to listen to language, and also privileges listening over speaking. In "The Way to Language," he even suggests that listening to language may be the fullest kind of speech, since it allows words to say what they could not otherwise say.

"Language first of all and inherently obeys the essential nature of speaking: it says . . .," Heidegger writes in "The Way to Language"; "What it says wells up from the formerly spoken and so far still unspoken Saying which pervades the design of language. . . . We, accordingly, listen to language in this way, [when] we let it say its Saying to us" (124). Heidegger, however, does not regard listening to language as an end in and of itself. He privileges this auditory activity, rather, as the "way" to something else: to appropriation or *Ereignis*. Heidegger also demonstrates in several of the other essays from *On the Way to Language*, if not in the title essay, that there are advantages inherent in listening to the language of others, as well as our own. Finally, he consistently characterizes appropriation in visual terms: it is the enabling of "radiant appearance" (126), a letting be seen (122), or—most often—a showing.

THE REVOLVING DIALOGUE

The notion of a "revolving dialogue" implies at least the possibility of a reciprocal activity on the part of the listener to that of the speaker, and so makes out of the transference something much more potentially social than it is usually assumed to be. Elsewhere in *Seminar I*, Lacan opens up his theoretical model even further. In a crucial passage earlier in that text, he generalizes the category of the transference to include all situations in which one person speaks in genuine cognizance that another is listening. He also suggests that such speech can be transformative of the listener as well as the speaker. "In its essence," Lacan writes there, "the efficacious transference which we're considering is quite simply the speech act. Each time a man speaks to another in an authentic and full manner, there is, in the true sense, transference. . . . something takes place which changes the nature of the two beings present" (109).

We have seen how the transference can transform the speaker, but not how it can transform the listener. As long as we conceptualize that event in psychoanalytic terms, the countertransference provides us with our primary model for conceiving of auditory

change. However, Lacan invites us here to conceptualize the transference outside psychoanalytic parameters. Surprising as it may
seem, in the already quoted passage in which he compares full
speech to a theatrical event, he also helps us to do just that. This is
because what begins as a simple analogy to the analytic situation
quickly develops into a rich meditation upon another of the crucial
domains within which a revolving discourse can occur and where
the world itself is always centrally at issue: the aesthetic. Significantly, this account of listening conforms much more closely to the
Heideggerian than to the Lacanian paradigm:

[The analysand correctly brings back] into present time the origins of his
own person. And he does this in a language that allows his discourse to be
understood by his contemporaries, and which furthermore presupposes
their present discourse. Thus it happens that the recitation of the *epos* may
include a discourse of earlier days in its own archaic, even foreign language, or may even pursue its course in present time with all the animation of the actor; but it is like an indirect discourse, isolated in quotation
marks within the thread of the narration, and, if the discourse is played
out, it is on a stage implying the presence not only of the chorus, but also
of spectators. (46–47)

At first, Lacan's dramatic analogy seems entirely calculated to
advance our understanding of the ideal analytical situation; as in
every "good" comparison, the metaphoric term is apparently at the
service of the literal term. In full speech, we learn, as in a particular
kind of theatrical event, what is spoken manifests itself as a constellation of signifiers rather than as a live event. The speaker speaks in
a way that reveals his words to be a repetition of what has been said
before, whether in symptom or verbal utterance. The one who effects this distantiation does not do so from a relation of exteriority
to his discourse. He does not assume his history, and then speak in
"quotation marks." Rather, his words return in that form from the
place of the Other.

However, before long, the vehicle of the theatrical metaphor
can be seen to exceed its tenor in a number of important respects.
First, with the invocation of a theatrical performance, Lacan directs

attention away from those strictly private forms of repetition through which the subject is integrated into the symbolic order to a fundamentally social transaction, where the point of address is not the Other, but a collectivity of others. There are also two different collectivities of others here: the chorus and the spectators. Only one of them—the chorus—can be structurally likened to the analyst, in that it, too, might be said to perform a "punctuating"[35] function with respect to the speaker's discourse. The spectators have no literal equivalent. They are thus a term in radical excess of the comparison Lacan draws.

This excessive term assumes, moreover, a centrally structuring role. With his insistence that the actor speak in a language "that allows his discourse to be understood by his contemporaries, and which furthermore presupposes their present discourse," Lacan reminds us that every speech which is worthy of the appellation, whether it be verbal or libidinal, is in dialogue not only with another subject, but also with an abstract language system. Listening thus not only comes to represent the site at which the signifier is graspable as such, but also the untranscendable horizon of *langue*. Lacan also suggests that the imperative of intelligibility properly governs the theatrical event at every stage, from its planning to its presentation.

This does not mean, however, that the audience constitutes a fixed paradigm, to which the speaker must conform himself. *Langue* does not in this case represent the synchronic dimension of language, and *parole* the diachronic.[36] Lacan twice temporalizes the discursive norm which speaking must respect. The abstract language system to which the actor must at least to some degree conform his words is "contemporar[y]" or "present." It is thus apparently one which mutates over time, presumably in response to the pressure of *parole*. To speak intelligibly also does not mean to speak exactly as others are speaking at the same moment. It means, rather, to speak *in relation* to the contemporary *langue*. Lacan makes clear how wide a latitude the notion of speaking in relation to the present discourse of one's contemporaries implies when he suggests that it may be satisfied even by someone speaking in an "archaic" or "foreign" language.

Since it has traditionally been more within the aesthetic than within the therapeutic context that "foreign" words have come into their own, this last feature of exemplary speech seems once again to have more pertinence for the tenor than for the vehicle of Lacan's metaphor. What begins as an analogy between full speech and the theatrical is thus beginning to seem more and more like a clarification of what distinguishes the theatrical event from its psychoanalytic counterpart. But we have not yet learned everything this passage has to tell us about aesthetic listening.

Heidegger refers often in "The Way to Language" to the kind of "saying" which "shows."[37] Lacan also attributes to speech the capacity to show in the passage under discussion; he characterizes those who hear the actor's speech not as "listeners," but rather as "spectators," as if to suggest that through this speech they are made to see something. For both authors, the notion of a "showing saying" seems to represent in part a useful catechresis through which to foreground something about language which language itself works to conceal.

When we speak, we usually hear the words we utter. We are therefore under the impression that we know what we are saying. We also think of hearing as something we do after the utterance of speech, and in response to it. When we show something, on the other hand, we often cannot see what we show. "Showing" also designates an activity which derives its meaning and raison d'être from its relation to a spectator. It is an action which we perform only when another is present, and *for* that other. In both of these ways, showing seems to incline much more precipitously toward the spectator than speaking does toward the listener. By characterizing saying as a showing, however, Lacan suggests that it, too, has this function—that it, too, finds its realization in the one to whom it is addressed rather than in the one who speaks.

But the word "spectator" is not merely a metaphor for "listener" in the passage under discussion. No matter how non-visual or negating the form it takes, every work of art begins and ends with an act of visual affirmation.[38] It begins when one subject allows a perceptual phenomenon to body forth beauty, and it ends when a second subject finds beauty in the same image, whether for the same or a different reason. Both artist and audience are definitionally spectators because art is in its irreducible essence the externalization and collectivization of something which is normally to be found only in the psychic encounter of a singular look with a perceptual phenomenon: an appearance. Sometimes what a work of art allows to appear in this dialogical way is a person, a color, or a thing. Sometimes it is simply itself.

When Lacan invokes as part of the exemplary theatrical performance the use of "archaic" or "foreign" words, he foregrounds another crucial difference between psychoanalysis and art. Psychoanalysis can only achieve its end by bringing us to ourselves—by making us the speakers of the word which is our own. Art functions in a radically different way. It achieves its end only by making us more cosmopolitan or "worldly" spectators—spectators capable of looking from a "there" which is not our own, even when it seems anachronistic or alien. As should be evident by now, to look from a "there" which is not one's own is also to care from a "there" which is not one's own. The real or metaphoric listener is thus the site at which the aesthetic work is realized in an even more profound sense than I have so far suggested; this work fulfills itself as such through the communication not merely of a visual phenomenon, but also of affect, from one subject to another. But the distinction is finally an empty one. To look—as I will attempt to demonstrate in the next two chapters—*is* to care.

HOLDING OPEN THE OPEN REGION OF THE WORLD

Although its locus is finally more the listener than the speaker, art might finally seem merely another of the names, like "clearing" or *manque-à-être*, for the opening up of a disclosive space. However, this is not exactly the case. Art does not "open," but "[clear] the openness of the Open" (62), as Heidegger puts it in "The Origin of the Work of Art." It does not create space but "[make] space for that spaciousness" which is gathered in the "world's worlding" (45). It does not free, but "liberate the [free of the] Open," and "establish it in its structure" (45).

I suggested at the beginning of the last chapter that *Dasein* is more an action than an entity. I want to propose in closing this chapter that the same can be said of the work of art: it, too, is more an action than an artifact. The action which *Dasein* performs and the action which art performs have one crucial thing in common: both are form-giving. Art making, like the creation of values in which each of us daily participates, shapes, molds, and sculpts. However, these activities are not identical. Through care, *Dasein* conjures the world out of the void, makes something out of nothing. Art, on the other hand, creates a structure within which the clearing which is created through care can be both exteriorized and protected. It "holds open" the "Open of the world" so that it can be apprehended as such (45). The work of art might be said to build a garden around the house of Being, and—in so doing—make it what it could not otherwise be: a site to which other men and women may journey to look.

We might be tempted to make a distinction here between the "master" of the abode, and those who only stay for a while. By enclosing his "thereness" in an external structure, is not the artist finally in a position to take possession of it?[39] In fact, I would argue, the artist is as much a visitor to this dwelling as are those who are only passing through. The space which makes room for the spaciousness which he might be said to "be" is one which he enters only through an alienating exstasis. As with the analysand, the moment at which the artist assumes his creative faculties, in the strongest sense of the word, is also the moment at which he surrenders them:[40] the moment when, rather than speaking and showing, he is looking and listening.

Once again, the lesson is unambiguous. In "owning," we are carried away from ourselves. It is our essence to be appropriated.

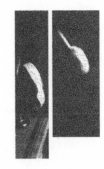

4

APPARATUS FOR THE
PRODUCTION OF AN IMAGE

To see is to have seen. . . . A seer has always already seen. Having
seen in advance he sees into the future. He sees the future tense
out of the perfect.
—Martin Heidegger, "The Anaximander Fragment"

Be not afeard; the isle is full of noises,
Sounds, and sweet airs, that give delight and hurt not.
Sometimes a thousand twangling instruments
Will hum about mine ears, and sometimes voices
That, if I then had waked after long sleep,
Will make me sleep again; and then in dreaming,
The clouds methought would open and show riches
Ready to drop upon me, that when I waked,
I cried to dream again.
—William Shakespeare, *The Tempest*, 3.2.138–46

In the preceding two chapters, I suggested that it is through
speaking our particular language of desire that we facilitate the appearance of other creatures and things. How can this be? Until now,
I have proposed no model other than a linguistic one for conceptu-

alizing speech. Although I referred in various passages to the "libidinal speech act," I defined such a speech act by means of two Saussurean categories: as the concrete realization and the at least potential individuation of an abstract *langue*.[1] But to appear is to become visible, or—as the *Oxford English Dictionary* alternately puts it—to "[come] forward into view."[2] The linguistic signifier can consequently have only a metaphoric relation to this all-important event.

In fact, although I have been using the term *langue* to refer to the abstract language system we draw upon when we engage in libidinal speech acts and *parole* to refer to such speech acts themselves, I am not conceptualizing either of those things according to a linguistic model. Kinship is not in my view equivalent in any way to the abstract language system of German, French, or English. The *langue* of each of these natural languages consists of a highly conventionalized and reasonably stable network of mutually defining terms. The word *mother* does not signify the same thing for every native English speaker, or even for the same person over an extended period of time, but it signifies enough of the same thing so that when one speaker utters the word another native English speaker can understand her. Within kinship, on the other hand, almost everything is in constant flux. A signifier means only through reference to a mnemonic constellation whose meaning it has itself helped to transform, and into which it will subsequently be assimilated.

Things are so semantically labile within kinship that we would have to refer to the libidinal speech act as an utterance devoid of a *langue* were it not for one thing: virtually everyone within the same culture begins speaking kinship by displacing away from one or more of an extremely limited set of familial terms, most classically one which is either maternal or paternal. It is, moreover, only so long as this familial term remains in its originating position that libidinal speech is possible. The *langue* of kinship is nothing more than this simple imperative.

This last assertion may run counter to the experience most of us have had of kinship, which is of a series of binding and coercive prescriptions. Nevertheless, it is not at the level of the abstract system of kinship that the elaborate codes and conventions which regulate our object-choices are elaborated. It is, rather, at the level of our libidinal speech. Wherever such codes and conventions govern, conforming a subject's language of desire to cultural norms, it is to what Heidegger calls the "they" that we must refer them.[3] We feel these codes and conventions as a coercive force because it is this "they," rather than we ourselves, who is speaking at the level of our desire.

Of course the pressure to invest libidinally in representations of the sort that constitute "mother" and "father" for other people makes itself felt from the very beginning of life. As soon as a small child can understand language or read the codes of dress, food, decor, and other domestic arrangements, she begins to learn a particular way of speaking kinship. However, in our present culture, what thereby takes hold of the child's desires is often less what might be called the language of the land than a "subcultural dialect," or even a highly individual "idiolect." She enters the world perhaps with two mothers and no father; with one father and the father's male lover, to whom she gives a name of purely private significance; or with a mother who works in a law firm, and a father who takes care of the home. It is not until several years later, when this child enters kindergarten, that she learns what a nuclear family is "supposed" to be. Yet during the intervening period she is far from being outside kinship; long before her first day at school, she has acceded to the incest taboo and has perhaps even effected her first displacement away from the mother to a pet dog.

The "they" does not even necessarily begin ventriloquizing this hypothetical child's desire at the moment that she comes home from school with the newly learned word "father," or "mother," wanting to know if she, too, has such a parent. Like any other speech act, a libidinal speech act must be enunciated. However, a libidinal speech act is no more equivalent to a verbal speech act than the *langue* of kinship is to that of a natural language. We signify libidinally not by producing sounds or making graphic notations, but rather by producing images; not by speaking or writing, but rather by looking.

It is therefore not until our imaginary child is able to make a metaphoric or metonymic link between a privileged unconscious memory and a perceptual stimulus in the present that she will be able to open up her language of desire to accommodate the alien familial term. Perhaps this will never happen. Perhaps, rather than effecting a visual condensation between the sable coat of her beloved collie and the rust jacket of a school mate's father one afternoon after school, thereby instilling in her a new appreciation for male musculature, this child will simply rediscover her mother's elegance in the movements of her first-grade school teacher.

The basic drive in the human subject is the urge to see once more what has been seen before. Kinship creates the unconscious by alienating this drive from the possibility of satisfaction and setting in place the imperative to displace. As its derivation would suggest, desire is as inextricably bound to the look as is the drive. It could be defined as the imperative to look in new places for what one seeks to see again: to see the old in a different guise. It is because it is primarily at the level of vision that we apprehend what was in what is that the passion of every subject's signifier is conducive of the appearance of certain creatures and things.

A PSYCHOANALYSIS WHICH IS NOT ONE

In asserting the psychic primacy of vision, I would seem to be breaking with the teachings of psychoanalysis. Although Freud acknowledges the predominantly visual status of the unconscious signifier,[4] and consistently maintains the priority for subjectivity of unconscious signification,[5] he does not seem prepared to grant the image even an equal psychic importance to the word.

In Chapter 2 of *Interpretation of Dreams*, Freud advances his famous definition of the discursive form to whose examination that book is devoted. A dream, he writes, is "*a (disguised) fulfilment of a (suppressed or repressed) wish*" (4: 160; Freud's emphasis). With this definition, Freud suggests that, far from being the result of a digestive process or a simple projection away from postural positionality, the sounds and images which pass with such hallucinatory intensity before us when we sleep tell us the truth about ourselves. From them we can learn what we could never otherwise know: what it is that we desire. However, this lesson is unavailable so long as we attribute perceptual value to what we see and hear. We can approach the truth of our desire only by grasping the sounds and images of our dreams as simple stand-ins or ciphers for what cannot be directly spoken. Freud might thus be said to derealize the manifest content of the dream.

Not surprisingly, in the pages that follow Freud always moves quickly away from the images and sounds of the dreams he analyzes to what they disguise. Neither the visual particularity of a given dream image nor the startling form in which a parental figure or an infantile object might be reconstituted there seems significant in its own right. Indeed, Freud encourages us to treat dream images as parts of a rebus, rather than as something at which it is intrinsically pleasurable to look. "If we attempted to read [the visual] characters [of a dream] according to their pictorial value instead of according to their symbolic relations, we should clearly be led into error," Freud writes in *Interpretation of Dreams*; "we can only form a proper judgment . . . if . . . we try to replace each separate element by a syllable or word that can be represented by that element in some way or other" (4: 277–78).

Freud also tells us in chapter 5 of his dream book that the dream work translates the predominantly verbal memories which he calls the "dream-thoughts" into perceptions only out of "considerations of representability" (5: 339–49). Images, he maintains, serve the requirements of condensation better than words, since their meaning is always multivalent. For the same reason, images also aid the censoring mechanism, which seeks to conceal the motivating desires behind our dreams; where the possibilities for meaning are many, a forbidden one can be easily hidden.

In other Freudian texts, vision serves not merely an instrumental, but also a pathological function; it emerges as something like the "disease" for which language provides the "cure." In treating the patients whose case studies form *Studies on Hysteria*, Freud tells us, he at times used language not only to neutralize the trauma of visual hallucinations, but also to erase the memory on the part of a patient that she had at one time even had such a hallucination.[6] Freud's case histories of Dora, little Hans, and the Wolfman all feature prominent examples of what might be called "visual symptoms," and in each of these texts the author elaborates further upon the notion of the "talking cure."[7] And in *Beyond the Pleasure Principle*, Freud celebrates the capacity of verbal speech to "bind" the trauma of nightmares which would otherwise compulsively return.[8]

However, as psychoanalysis teaches us, it is not from consciousness, ostensible seat of knowledge, that we finally have the most to learn. It is, rather, from the Other whom each of us might finally be said to be. This Other, who does not seem to think that the dream-work produces images only out of considerations of representability, speaks eloquently from the site of Freud's own dreams. Both in these dreams and in the dream thoughts out of which they emerge, the activity of looking occupies an extraordinarily privileged position.

In Freud's dream of Irma's injection, for instance, he plays the role of a diegetic as well as an extradiegetic observer.[9] In it, he looks down the throat of Irma, one of his hysterical patients, and peruses a spectacle which is clearly the product of a lavish amount of dream work: "extensive whitish grey scabs upon some remarkable curly structures which were evidently modeled on the turbinal bones of the nose" (4: 107). Freud invites Dr. M. to join him in front of this spectacle, and shortly thereafter two more male colleagues collect around Irma as well, forming a grouping as theatrically scopic as any ever staged by Charcot. The men soon extend their visual inspection beyond Irma's throat to her shoulders. In spite of the fact that she is fully clothed, they are able to detect an "infiltration" in the skin.

In his analysis of this dream, Freud evokes a peculiar visual memory of a former patient: the discovery in the mouth of a beautiful governess of unsightly dentures (4: 109). He tells us that this discovery, which the governess attempted to forestall by not open-ing her mouth, was the source of dissatisfaction not only to the governess but also to Freud himself. But although Freud locates the figure of the governess behind Irma, who also seems reluctant to open her mouth, his account of the dream thoughts does not en-courage us to read the dream as a restaging of this particular visual memory. Rather, Freud intimates in it that the dream of Irma's in-jection was inspired by the desire to look at a very different part of the female body from the oral cavity. I say "intimates" because the author of *Interpretation of Dreams* manifests a curious reluctance to acknowledge what his own analysis demonstrates.

We do not expect coyness from Freud on such matters. He quite unabashedly shares with us not only the concealed thought whereby he makes his friend Otto responsible for Irma's illness (the thought, that is, that the infusion on Irma's shoulder must have come from an injection given to her by him [4: 117]), but also the double entendre by means of which this medical infraction be-comes a sexual infraction: "*And probably the syringe had not been clean*" (4: 118; Freud's emphasis). However, in the passage in which Freud glosses the words behind which his scopic desire lies con-cealed—"in spite of her dress"—he comes up against the force of his own resistance to the analysis. The result is consequently not a simple declarative, but rather a negation—an avowal through de-nial:[10] "We naturally used to examine the children in the hospital undressed," Freud writes, "and this would be a contrast to the man-ner in which adult female patients have to be examined. I remem-bered that it was said of a celebrated clinician that he never made a physical examination of his patients except through their clothes. Further than this I could not see. Frankly, I had no desire to pene-trate more deeply at this point" (4: 113).

But this is not all in Freud's account of the dream of Irma's in-jection to connect it with a passionate scopophilia. In the course of discussing the contents of Irma's mouth, the author of *Interpreta-tion of Dreams* remarks that "there is at least one spot in every dream at which it is unplumbable—a navel, as it were, that is its point of contact with the unknown" (4:111, footnote). Much later in the same book, Freud adds that this spot marks the location of the (presumably primary) dream wish (5: 525). He attributes the un-plumbability of the dream navel to the thicketlike density of dream thoughts surrounding it, thoughts which branch out in too many directions to admit of an exhaustive interpretation (5: 525).[11]

Freud finds the navel of the dream of Irma's injection in Irma herself. Concealed behind this figure, he tells us, were his wife, his daughter, and a friend of Irma.[12] Surprisingly, however, he does not support the claim that Irma represents the navel of the dream by underscoring the abyssal nature of the dream thoughts out of which she was formed. Rather, Freud says that he is not able to give us an exhaustive account of Irma's meaning because he didn't push his in-terpretation far enough. He did not do so because exploring the ideational motivations for the condensation of his wife, his daugh-ter, and Irma's friend into this single, composite figure would have taken him "far afield" (4.111, footnote). With these last words, he himself comes close to acknowledging what we have already sur-mised: his mention of Irma's hybrid construction in the footnote is a false lead. Far from representing a crucial moment in the analytic undoing of repression, this revelation is itself part and parcel of that process of censorship through what is of secondary importance is pushed to the foreground, and what is of primary importance is concealed in the background.

But although Freud himself misidentifies the navel of the dream of Irma's injection, he makes it possible for us to rectify his mistake. In his analysis of the words "in spite of her dress," he provides the missing trope of unplumbability. He thereby indicates that it is these words which mark the "point of contact with the unknown" in this "specimen dream" of psychoanalysis.[13] One of the two sen-tences following the one in which Freud refers to the celebrated phy-sician who always examined his patients fully clothed—"frankly, I had no desire to penetrate more deeply at this point"—also helps us to understand that if Freud's dream escapes interpretation at this crucial point, this is not because of an overdetermination of meaning. It is, rather, because the wish of the dreamer not to see what he is seeing is as strong as his desire to see.

Freud's dream of the botanical monograph is even more saturated with visual longing, but here the force of denial is not nearly as powerful.[14] This dream consists in its entirety of a single act of vision. In it, Freud dreams that a book devoted to a botanical topic is lying before him, and that he is turning over one of its colored plates (4: 169). Other books with colored plates figure prominently in the dream thoughts out of which the botanical monograph dream emerges. Freud speaks of the passion he had for such books during his days as a medical student. He was, we learn, "*enthralled*" by their images (4: 172; my emphasis). This memory leads to another, in which Freud and his sister as children disassembled books with colored plates. Again, this memory is generative of extreme pleasure; "bliss" (ibid.) is the word with which Freud characterizes it. The author of *Interpretation of Dreams* tells us that the "picture" of this act of destruction was the only "plastic memory" he retained from his childhood, further underscoring both its visual consistency and its importance (ibid.).

The motivating incident for the dream of the botanical monograph was the spectacle of a botanical monograph in a shop window (4: 169). This spectacle reminded Freud that he, too, once wrote a kind of botanical monograph, a book on the coca plant (4: 170). Lest we imagine for a moment that this last memory, at least, has no visual ramifications, Freud tells us that it immediately gave rise to a fantasy of eye surgery, whereby he was delivered, with the help of cocaine, from an imaginary case of glaucoma (ibid.).

Finally, Freud isolates as the most important wish behind the dream of the botanical monograph the desire to see *Interpretation of Dreams* "lying finished before [him]" (4: 172). He attributes the inspiration for the dream wish to two sentences from a letter recently written to him by Fliess: "I am very much occupied with your dream-book. *I see it lying finished before me and I see myself turning over its pages*" (ibid.; Freud's emphasis). However, the formulation through which Freud expresses the dream wish makes evident how much resonance Fliess's scopic fantasy found within his own psyche: "How much I envied [Fliess] his gift as a seer! If only I could have seen it lying finished before me!"(ibid.).

In Freud's dream of self-dissection, he not only once again functions as a diegetic as well as an extradiegetic spectator, he also provides the spectacle at which he looks. In this dream, his former teacher old Brücke sets him the task of helping Louise N. to dissect his own pelvis. Freud performs this task primarily through looking at his own anatomy. What he sees appeals strongly to his aesthetic faculties, inviting him to distinguish between background and foreground, the sculptural and the painterly, and the natural and the cultural: "I [see my pelvis and legs] before me," he writes. "The pelvis ha[s] been eviscerated, and it [is] visible now in its superior, now in its inferior, aspect, the two being mixed together. Thick flesh-colored protuberances . . . [can] be seen.[15] Something which lay over it and was like crumpled silver-paper had also to be carefully fished out" (5: 452).

At a certain point in his dream of self-dissection, Freud leaves the operating room where he scrutinizes his pelvis and is carried toward a small wooden house. At this point, he is seemingly subsumed completely to the role of invalid, no longer functioning as a spectacle in relation to his own look. In fact, however, this part of the dream attests as fully as the earlier part to a narcissistic scopophilia. Freud attributes the detail of the wooden house to his desire to be buried at some future moment in an Etruscan grave (5: 454–55). In "The Future of an Illusion," he returns to this dream, now explicitly connecting it to his love of ancient visual artefacts. It is, moreover, no longer simply his desire to be buried in an Etruscan grave which he represents the dream as fulfilling; Freud maintains that the dream also satisfied his desire to *see* himself lying in such a grave.[16]

But Freud's dreams are not the only elements in *Interpretation of Dreams* attesting to the psychic centrality of the look. The model of the psyche to which that work is committed is at every point a visual model.

THE PSYCHE AS AN OPTICAL DEVICE

The psyche, Freud tells us in a famous passage from *Interpretation of Dreams*, resembles "a compound microscope or a photographic apparatus" (5: 536). At first, the basis for this comparison seems fairly minor. Psychic images, like those inside these two optical devises, are "virtual" rather than real; they occur at sites where no "tangible component" of the apparatus is located. But a page later, we learn that there is another ground for the analogizing of psyche and camera, if not psyche and microscope. The various systems which constitute the psyche stand in a regular relation to each other, like the lenses in a camera. Excitation passes through these systems in a particular order, just as light does through the photographic lenses.

Immediately below the passage quoted above, the author of *Interpretation of Dreams* maintains that a psychical locality "correspond[s]" to "a point inside the apparatus at which one of the preliminary stages of an image comes into being" (5: 536). With the vehicle of this metaphor, Freud stresses the teleological aspect of a photographic apparatus. A camera, he suggests, is not only a spatial organization through which light passes, but also a temporal process whose end is the production of an image. The German verb with which Freud links the vehicle of his metaphor to the tenor, and which Strachey translates with the English word *correspond,* is *entsprechen,*[17] which is suggestive of more than simple similarity; it means "to be equivalent to," "to conform to," or "to be commensurate with." If psychical locality corresponds to the camera in the way Freud specifies, it, too, must be the site for the emergence of what might be called "a picture in the making." The psyche in its entirety, like the camera, must also constitute a temporal process whose pregiven end point is the realization of this picture.

A psychical locality is the site for a preliminary stage in the making of an image rather than for the appearance of an image as such because it represents a memory system. Freud is at great pains to establish that perception occurs in a "place" apart from memory.

In *Interpretation of Dreams*, as in *Beyond the Pleasure Principle* and "A Note upon the 'Mystic Writing-Pad,'" he maintains that the psyche is divided between two incommensurate activities: perception and memory. Where we receive sensory stimuli, we cannot store them. Conversely, where we store them, we cannot receive them.[18]

Both the unconscious and the preconscious are psychical localities.[19] However, memories are inscribed in a very different form in each of these localities. Unconscious memories are perceptions—and specifically visual perceptions—in potentia. They aspire to become what Freud calls "thing-presentations," that is, representations which are capable of passing themselves off as things.[20] Preconscious memories, on the other hand, are linguistic in nature, consisting of verbal signifiers and conceptual signifieds. Freud refers to these memories, which are subject to other forms of differentiation as well, as "word-presentations."[21]

Perception, which is not a locality, constitutes another psychic division. Freud attributes it to different but interfacing agencies in *Interpretation of Dreams*: to what he calls "perception" and to what he calls "consciousness." In the final diagram there with which he schematizes the psychic apparatus, Freud relegates these two parts of what he will later call the "perception/consciousness system"[22] to opposite ends of the psychic apparatus.[23] Intervening between them are the unconscious and the preconscious (see figure).

The perception part of the perception/consciousness system is not perception proper, but merely the unconscious psychic registration of an external stimulus. Before a perceptual stimulus can become conscious, and so be truly perceived, it must coalesce with an unconscious memory or cluster of memories. This coalescence, which Freud calls "perceptual identity,"[24] may be effected through the condensation of perceptual stimulus and unconscious memory. It may also be effected through a libidinal displacement from the unconscious memory to the perceptual stimulus. In both cases, though, the perceptual moment within this process of identification takes place within the consciousness part of the perception/consciousness system.[25] Because consciousness is for Freud nothing

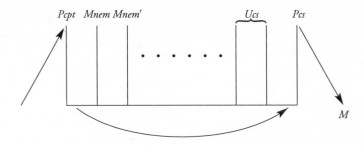

more than the site at which our psychically worked-over perceptions become available to us, he does not hesitate to characterize it as a sensory organ.[26]

Freud not only compares the psyche to an optical apparatus in *Interpretation of Dreams*; he also provides an emphatically specular gloss upon his revolutionary definition of a dream. In chapter 7 of that work, he tells us again, once more in italics, that a dream is a disguised fulfillment of a suppressed or repressed wish. However, he now adds a new criterion to the desire out of which a dream can emerge. In addition to being prohibited, this desire must be of a visual or "scenic" nature. A dream, Freud writes, is "*a substitute for an infantile scene modified by being transferred on to a recent experience. The infantile scene is unable to bring about its own revival and has to be content with returning as a dream*" (5: 546).

Strangely, moreover, Freud here personifies the infantile scene: it is the one seeking to bring about its own revival and it is the one which must be content to return in another form. This is not the only time Freud imputes something like subjectivity to our visual memories. He reverts repeatedly in *Interpretation of Dreams* to a peculiar verbal formula. He suggests that our unconscious memories exercise a powerful force of "attraction" over our other thoughts and perceptions.

The first time Freud attributes to the unconscious memories a capacity to attract he seems to be simply anticipating a claim which he will later make in "Repression," which is that when something is repressed it is not merely repelled by the preconscious, but attracted by the unconscious.[27] However, a few pages later he suggests that the *visual properties* of the unconscious memories have an important part to play in the event he is describing. The "transformation of thoughts into visual images" in our dreams, Freud writes, "may be in part the result of the attraction which memories couched in visual form and eager for revival bring to bear upon thoughts cut off from consciousness and struggling to find expression" (5: 546).

The German word which Strachey translates as "attraction" is *die Anziehung*,[28] which can signify either an attribute or an action. It can designate the charms which a person or a thing has for others; or it can signify a pulling on the part of that person or thing of other people or things toward it. Freud seems to be using *die Anziehung* here in both senses. The dream thoughts, which are primarily verbal in form, find the predominantly imagistic qualities of the unconscious memories fascinating. The unconscious memories flaunt these qualities, in the hope of drawing the dream thoughts in their direction. The first of these interpretations makes evident, once again, how central the visual is to our psychic existence. The second does even more: it imputes to the unconscious memories a kind of agency. Those memories seem, indeed, to be the site of a certain desire—of a desire for what might be called "affiliation."

But if unconscious memories flaunt their visual properties at night, in an attempt to lure words into assuming a visual consistency, it is they themselves who go in search of visual stimuli when the door to the outside world is open. Freud explains this phenomenon through the concept of attention in *Project for a Scientific Psychology*. Attention, he suggests, is not the condition of conscious alertness which we usually think of it as being. Rather, it is the sending out of "wishful . . . cathexis . . . to meet all perceptions, since those that are wished-for might be among them."[29] What is wished for is a perception with which a visual memory can coalesce (4: 361). The one doing the wishing is again seemingly that memory itself, which seeks to make itself seen once more. What interests this memory in perception is precisely what it itself lacks: "perceptual quality" (4: 309).

Whether they draw verbal memories toward them, or go out in search of sensory stimuli, the unconscious memories seem to be driven by the desire to become conscious perceptions, a desire which they can realize only by finding a new shape. In waking life, they achieve this metamorphosis by coalescing with perceptual stimuli. During sleep, they achieve it by inducing verbal memories to provide an analogous visual habitus. If, in trying to make sense of this strange account of unconscious memories, I am unable to avoid attributing to them the status of a subject, that is because subjectivity itself is in its most profound sense nothing other than a constellation of visual memories which is struggling to achieve a perceptual form.

THE PLEASURE PRINCIPLE

It is not only because of the centrality which this model of the psyche affords the visual that it must be attributed to "another" Freud. The passages in which Freud elaborates it also defy the usual logic of attribution because making sense of them requires a completely different understanding of the pleasure principle than the one explicitly put forth in *Interpretation of Dreams* and *Beyond the Pleasure Principle*. According to the latter text, the pleasure principle represents the urge to reduce psychic excitation—which derives in part from external stimuli, but more fully from unsatisfied drives—to a level "as low as possible" (9).[30] At the beginning of life, when this principle reigns supreme, we seek not only to evacuate such excitation, but to do so as quickly as possible. Freud maintains that for this reason the psyche is a "reflex apparatus."[31] Although a reflex action is one which returns to its point of origin, Freud does not seem to be using it in that sense, but more as a synonym for the drive to expel.

Since hallucination provides the shortest path to pleasure, it is initially the preferred solution to the problem of psychic excitation; when the infant subject is hungry, Freud tells us in *Interpretation of Dreams*, it simply converts the mnemonic image of milk into an immediate perception. Before long, though, the unwanted excitation makes itself felt once again, and over time, the subject learns to tolerate a certain amount of tension as the precondition for "thought." The goal of the "thinking" psyche nevertheless remains exactly the same as its "thoughtless" counterpart: it, too, operates at the behest of the pleasure principle. The only difference between the two is that the thinking psyche has learned to distinguish between fantasmatic discharge, and real discharge, and it knows that the path leading to the latter is generally more tortuous and circuitous than the path leading to the former.[32]

The optical apparatus model of the psyche contradicts this account of the pleasure principle in every respect. Not only does it represent the end toward which the psyche is driven as the emergence of an image, but it also specifies as the precondition for that event to occur a heightening rather than a diminution of excitement. Indeed, in order for perception to take place, not just one but two sources of stimulation must be present—one external or sensory, and one internal or mnemonic. In perception, Freud tells us,

Excitatory material flows in to the *Cs.* sense-organ from two directions, from the *Pcpt.* system, whose excitation, determined by qualities, is probably submitted to a fresh revision before it becomes a conscious sensation, and from the interior of the apparatus itself, whose quantitative processes are felt qualitatively in the pleasure-unpleasure series when, subject to certain modifications, they make their way into consciousness.[33]

The excitement elicited by the two stimuli mentioned by Freud is, moreover, not simply a kind of "fore-pleasure," which is at the service of an evacuatory "end-pleasure."[34] This excitation or "quantitative" force is not ultimately released. Rather, it is transformed into an affective judgment about the perceptual thing. A quantity in the subject is converted into a quality in the object.[35]

Near the end of *Interpretation of Dreams* comes another passage challenging the canonical account of the pleasure principle. In this passage, Freud subjects the concept of "discharge" to a radical resignification. "The primary process," he observes there, "endeavors to bring about a discharge of excitation in order that, with the help of the amount of excitation thus accumulated, it may establish a 'perceptual identity' [with the experience of satisfaction]" (5: 602). Here, "discharge" means not "release of psychic tension," but rather something like "transfer of libido from one memory to another for the purpose of allowing the second memory to take the place of the first"—"displacement," in other words. It designates, that is, not the evacuation of excitation from the psyche into the exterior, but rather its circulation within a closed system. Discharge is also a process without any logical terminus; libido is no sooner removed from one memory than it is invested in another, which itself releases its cathexis only so that it can be located in a third, and so on. Finally, perceptual identity does not lead to discharge; rather, it is that to which discharge itself leads. Through the displacement of excitation away from one memory to a perceptual stimulus or another memory, the latter comes to have the perceptual "charge" of the former.

Since the transfer of libido from one term to another is something which occurs only when the drive to expel excitation from the psyche into the "outside" is blocked, it might nevertheless appear to represent more the frustration than the fulfilment of the pleasure principle. This is how Freud himself represents the matter in an important passage in *Beyond the Pleasure Principle*: "What appears in a minority of human individuals as an untiring impulsion towards further perfection," he writes in this passage,

> can easily be understood as a result of the instinctual repression upon which is based all that is most precious in human civilization. The repressed instinct never ceases to strive for complete satisfaction, which would consist in the repetition of a primary experience of satisfaction. No substitutive or reactive formations and no sublimations will suffice to remove the repressed instinct's persisting tension; and it is the difference in amount between the pleasure of satisfaction which is *demanded* and that which is actually *achieved* that provides the driving factor which will permit of no halting at any position attained, but, in the poet's words, '*ungebändigt immer vorwärts dringt*'" ['presses ever forward unsubdued']. (42)

However, Freud here openly acknowledges that it is the inhibition of the impulse toward energic evacuation which constitutes the driving force behind subjectivity. He also claims that the frustration of the urge to evacuate leads to the creation of "all that is most precious in human civilization." Freud thereby encourages us to understand the controlling principle of psychic life in a way that runs directly counter to his own definition of it.

On the basis of these three crucial irruptions of unconscious truth into Freud's iconoclastic discourse, I would like to suggest that the pleasure principle is not the nirvana principle which he himself claims it to be. It has nothing whatever to do either with a zero state of excitation or with the recovery of a lost satisfaction. Rather, the pleasure principle is psychoanalysis's name for what governs us psychically when we find our pleasure in *not* being satisfied—when we give ourselves over to the metonymical and metaphorical "slide" which leads away from, rather than back to, the ostensible point of origin.[36] The pleasure principle therefore does not triumph when we succeed in possessing again what we imagine ourselves once to have had, but rather when, through a series of associative connections, we succeed in representing what we yearn for in a new way.

I would also like to suggest that the pleasure principle does not constitute a generalized principle of repetition, but rather one which is specifically visual. The pleasure principle can best be defined as the enabling force behind a particular kind of looking: the kind of looking which is creative of beauty or preciousness. It is the impetus driving us to find visual gratification in perceptions that only imperfectly replicate our memories, and—in so doing—to ennoble ever new creatures and things. It is that to which we owe our capacity to affirm the phenomenal multiplicity of our earthly habitus: to become world spectators.

If the pleasure principle is what leads the subject from one visual signifier to another, rather than, as Freud at times maintains, a nearly physiological force pushing for a zero state of excitation, then it is clearly not something immanent within the newborn subject.

It must depend for its activation upon a symbolic rather than a biological agency. As I will attempt to demonstrate in the next chapter, that agency is kinship.

THE AGE OF THE WORLD PICTURE

The word which Freud consistently uses to refer to the image toward whose production the psyche moves is *Sachvorstellung*,[37] which James Strachey translates as "thing-presentation." With this translation, he succeeds in communicating the perceptual nature of psychic images. However, "thing-presentation" is in other respects a less than satisfactory translation of the original text. A compound noun, *Sachvorstellung* brings together one of a series of German words for "thing," *Sache*, with the semantically rich word *Vorstellung*, which can be translated as "presentation," "representation," "introduction," "performance," "idea," or "show," and which in its verbal form literally means "to position or stand before."

For the Heidegger of "The Age of the World Picture," the literal signification is the primary meaning of *Vorstellung*. This meaning makes manifest something which is at the heart of all representation: the aspiration on the part of the one who represents to order everything in relation to herself. To represent is not merely to set something "in place before oneself," and "to have it fixedly before oneself as set up in this way."[38] It is also to make of the one who looks "that being upon which all that is, is grounded as regards the manner of its Being and its truth"—to make of her the "center of that which is as such" (128).

The viewer I have just described is for Heidegger the modern or Cartesian subject. It is characteristic of this subject not merely to treat isolated phenomena in this way, but to regard the world itself as a picture. For the one for whom the world is a picture, writes Heidegger in the same essay, "an essential decision takes place regarding what is, in its entirety. The Being of whatever is, is sought and found in the representedness of the latter" (130). With this development, the category of the object—which constitutes, finally, a category of possession—emerges as such. Everything that I succeed in representing belongs to me, or should belong to me. It is mine (or should be mine) to do with as I see fit. It is, in other words, *for* me.

The language which Freud uses to describe the desire driving the dream of the botanical monograph—"If only *I* could have seen it lying finished before me!"—echoes to an uncanny degree the desire which Heidegger locates at the heart of modernity. Freud's dream of Irma's injection is vulnerable to the same critique. It attests powerfully to the subject/object binary which Heidegger locates at the heart of what he calls "the age of the world picture." Irma is not merely a convenient representation, for Freud, of a host of other women; she is, in addition, an object to be handled, manipulated, and known. The third dream which I discussed earlier in this chapter—the dream of self-dissection—also speaks to a desire for visual mastery. In it, Freud attempts to internalize the public look in relation to which his sexuality will be placed by the future publication of *Interpretation of Dreams* by consolidating *himself* as the one who looks at his private parts. Although vividly dramatizing the visual nature of desire, these three dreams are far from testifying to the generosity of the look.

For Mikkel Borch-Jacobsen, who has also noted the centrality of vision in Freud, the concept of the *Sachvorstellung* has no value other than the one Heidegger would impute to it. "If the 'content' of the unconscious is defined essentially as representation, as *Vorstellung* . . . can we avoid asking *in front of* what, in front of what 'agency,' this *Vor-stellung* is posited or presented? What is this psyche . . . unless it is, still and always a subject [of representation]?" he asks.[39] However, it does not follow from the primacy which Freud gives to the *Sachvorstellung* that we are all doomed to a constant reenactment of the *Cogito*. Borch-Jacobsen finds no descriptive value in Freud's account of the psyche. In his view, the dreamers whose dreams Freud recounts do not desire to *have* what they see; rather, they desire to *be* it.[40] At the moment that this mimetic desire is fulfilled, the spectator loses all distance from the scene of representation, and becomes purely and simply part of the picture. Consequently, the kind of "seeing" in which each of us engages in our dreams could not be farther removed from the kind Descartes inaugurated in the *Discourse on Method* and the *Meditations on First Philosophy.*

While I do not subscribe to the notion that Borch-Jacobsen succeeds where Freud fails, it does seem to me that he identifies another of the forms which the unconscious look can assume.[41] Clearly, there are times when each of us looks in an identificatory rather than a possessive way at what we see. However, I do not find in this expanded account of our spectatorial options much cause for celebration. Whereas the desire to possess expresses itself at the level of vision through the belong-to-be quality of certain kinds of representation,[42] mimetic desire classically expresses itself at the level of vision through the aspiration to incorporate the ideal image. It is, as Borch-Jacobsen himself makes clear, therefore the most altruicidal of all desires; it can achieve its end only by negating the other as such. "Mimesis is . . . the matrix of rivalry, hatred, and (in the social order) violence," he writes in *The Freudian Subject*; " 'I want what my brother, my model, my idol wants—and I want it in his place.' And, consequently, 'I want to kill him, to eliminate him' " (27).

Fortunately, although the relations of "being" and "having" have monopolized psychoanalytic attention to the virtual exclusion of any other, they do not constitute our only scopic options. As *Interpretation of Dreams* helps us to understand, the look can also relate to what it sees in the mode of *showing*. And when we *show* what we see, instead of seeking to replace it or take possession of it, the *Vorstellung* no longer has the status Heidegger imputes to it. Instead, it becomes coterminous with disclosure itself.

EXCITATION IN THE ORGAN OF VISION

Freud's account of the production of a perception often makes that process seem more exhibitionistic than scopophilic. The driving force behind perception appears to be the desire on the part of a past perception to make itself seen once again, rather than the desire on the part of a seer to see. *Interpretation of Dreams* seems to provide us with an unambiguous explanation for this desire to show. At several different moments in that text, Freud maintains that the dreamer herself always occupies the center of the scene. To be more precise, he writes that all dreams are "completely egoistic: the beloved ego appears in all of them, even though it may be disguised" (4: 267).[43] He thereby suggests that it is because it is primarily our own image which we seek to see in our dreams that the latter often seem more concerned with exhibiting than with seeing.

However, in chapter 7 of *Interpretation of Dreams* Freud makes a directly contrary claim. He compares the dreamer not to the hero of a story, but to the author of a play, and he goes so far as to insist that we are always aware in our dreams that we are performing this role (5: 571–72). The author of a play is generally a writer who composes with the aim of showing someone or something else. And in another passage in *Interpretation of Dreams*, Freud describes a kind of looking which also aims to show: a looking which helps what it sees realize itself as spectacle. He also implicitly opposes the pleasure which such looking provides to the pleasure entailed in looking at oneself.

"Scherner supposes that, when dreams exhibit particularly vivid and copious visual elements, there is present a state of 'visual stimulation,' that is, of internal excitation in the organ of vision," Freud writes at the beginning of this passage (5: 546). Although the words he utters derive from another author,[44] he goes on in the immediately following passage to signal his fundamental agreement with the latter's theoretical formulation. Freud then describes one of his own dreams. It is one which induced precisely that state of "visual stimulation" described by Scherner.

The dream in question is initially discussed in chapter 6 of *Interpretation of Dreams* (5: 463–68). It seems at first glance to provide so transparent an instantiation of the principle that our dreams are narcissistically motivated as to render interpretation superfluous. In it, Freud finds himself in a castle by a sea in which a naval battle is taking place. He is a volunteer naval officer, under the command of a governor. This governor, Herr P., dies quite suddenly, leaving a vacuum which only Freud can fill. He is thus implicitly promoted from lowly subordinate to commander in chief.

Surprisingly, though, in the interpretation which immediately follows, Freud reads the dream as a narrative of his own death, rather than that of Herr P. He does so by emphasizing the very substitutory logic which seems to work at the behest of narcissistic pleasure. "The analysis showed," writes Freud, ". . . that Herr P was only a substitute for my own self. (In the dream *I* was a substitute for *him*.) *I* was the Governor who suddenly died" (5: 464–65). At the same time, Freud traces the dream back to what he calls "the most cheerful recollections," recollections which are both emphatically visual, and decidedly worldly: "It was a year earlier, in Venice, and we were standing one magically beautiful day at the windows of our room on the Reva degli Schiavoni and were looking across the blue lagoon on which that day there was more movement than usual. English ships were expected and were to be given a ceremonial reception" (5: 465).

When Freud returns to the topic of this dream later in *Interpretation of Dreams*, he makes no reference to the role he himself played in it. Instead, he talks only about the pleasure of looking, which now seems to have been his primary experience not only on the day he stood gazing at the Riva degli Shiavoni, but also on the occasion of the dream itself. "What was it that had brought my visual organ into this state of stimulation?" Freud asks. His scopic excitation, he then explains, derived from the coalescence of an external perceptual stimulus with a series of earlier memories:

A recent impression, which attached itself to a number of earlier ones. The colors which I saw were in the first instance those of a box of toy bricks with which, on the day before the dream, my children had put up a fine building and shown it off for my admiration. The big bricks were of the same dark red and the small ones were of the same blue and brown. This was associated with color impressions from my last travels in Italy: the beautiful blue of the Isonzo and the lagoons and the brown of the Carso. (547)

Freud concludes this remarkable passage with the astonishing claim that "the beauty of the colors in my dream was only a repetition of something seen in my memory" (5: 547). In characteristic fashion, he cannot here "see" the manifest content of this dream, even though the pleasure he took in the latter clearly inhered in a very particular red, a very particular blue, and a very particular brown. Nevertheless, what Freud reveals to us here about his dream makes possible another account altogether of the kind of looking it entailed.

First, this dream would seem to fulfill in a very precise way the second formulation with which Freud defines a dream. In it, a cluster of scenes which are unable to bring about their own perceptual revival return in the guise of another. That the dream satisfies in a transformative guise the wish to see once again what has been seen before is concealed in Freud's original account of it. The marine setting in which the desired blue, red, and brown return evokes not pleasure in the dreamer, but rather "a tense and sinister impression" (5: 464) The affect has been turned into its opposite—"cheerfulness into fear" (5: 465). Freud attributes this affective reversal to the latent meaning signified by the colors in his dream, which presumably means the anticipation of his own death. However, in the later passage, the affective reversal has been undone. Not only does Freud openly acknowledge that the dream gave him a great deal of pleasure, but he also attributes that pleasure to the dream's images themselves, rather than to some nonvisual signified.

But this passage provides more than a vivid dramatization of the principle that it is above all the desire to *resee* that motivates our dreams. It also attests to the excitatory nature of visual pleasure. When Freud looks at the colors in his dream, he does not experience a release of tension. Rather, he is stimulated, and this stimulation brings pleasure. Freud's state of excitement is, moreover, creative of exciting things. The toy bricks which were the perceptual stimulus for Freud's dream become precious, or—as he himself puts it—beautiful. This passage thus dramatizes in a very precise way the change from the "quantitative" into the "qualitative."

Finally, the egoic death which Freud undergoes in this dream seems to be the precondition for the pleasure he takes in its visual signifiers. I qualify this death as "egoic" because it does not denote the end of Freud as subject, but rather the dissolution of that "mirage" which blinds him to who he is.[45] What might be called the "toy brick dream" is, in a sense, a call to desire: a solicitation to Freud to begin speaking his very particular language of desire, and—in so doing—to come to "himself." Freud does not hear this call. But at least in the brief period it took him to compose the sentences quoted above, he could be said to have looked not for his own sake, but rather for the sake of what looking makes possible: the appearance of creatures and things. He became a seer who passed over affectively to the side of what he saw.

Freud tells us that when we sleep, the door to the world is closed.[46] It would thus seem difficult to posit this dream as an instance of world spectatorship, as I have been implicitly doing. However, during the minutes or hours during which Freud exercised his creative faculties in the way I have just described, he was not asleep. Rather, he was dreaming while awake. And not only was the door to the world open, but Freud went through it. He returned, bearing gifts, to the perceptual stimulus with which the dream itself began: to the red, blue, and brown bricks with which his children constructed their "fine" building, which thereafter shimmered with the radiance of the Isonzo, the lagoons, and the Carso.

Now at last we are able to make sense of Freud's claim that the psychical apparatus is "constructed like a reflex apparatus." As long as we remain faithful to the notion that the pleasure principle decrees the evacuation of excitation, this is an inexplicable assertion. The accumulation of excitation at one end of the psychic apparatus and its release at the other does not constitute a reflex, which involves what the *Oxford English Dictionary* calls the "bending back" of something from whence it came.[47] However, once we understand the pleasure principle as the force behind perceptual identity, we have no difficulty in explaining its reflex nature. Insofar as the action which begins with the reception of a sensory stimulus in fact ends with the production of an image, it necessarily bends back toward the sensory stimulus itself. In so doing, it imparts to that stimulus what the latter could not otherwise have: psychic value. Something like a reflex arc also figures prominently in Heidegger's own account of the look.[48] It is the shape of care.[49]

My reader may therefore not be surprised to learn that the world is not in competition with our dreams. On the contrary, it intends toward the newness and braveness which they alone can provide. Much in the spirit of Caliban in *The Tempest*, the trees are murmuring to the brooks, and the birds to the clouds: "If this be sleep, let them go on dreaming."

5

THE MILKY WAY

It is, as I have argued, primarily by looking that we speak our language of desire. Our libidinal speech acts consequently consist more often of images than of words. But the look has chronological as well as affective priority over the word. Not only do we begin seeing before we can speak, but it is also due to a specifically visual imperative that we turn to language. Words are born out of our desire to make available to consciousness what would otherwise remain fully beyond our knowledge: what we have already seen and what we hope yet to see.

We cannot minimize the force of this challenge to our customary logocentrism simply by putting the image in the place classically reserved for the word, since we do not enunciate visually in the same way as we enunciate verbally. The linguistic signifier is prototypically closed: closed to affective transfers, closed to other linguistic signifiers, and closed to the world. The perceptual signifier, on the other hand, is open: open to affective transfers, open to other perceptual signifiers, and open to the world. It is because of these differences that appearance is primarily a visual, rather than a verbal, event.

PROLEGOMENON TO A THEORY OF THE PERCEPTUAL SIGNIFIER

In appendix C of Freud's 1914 essay "The Unconscious," which consists of an early essay on aphasia, he provides us with the two most crucial categories for conceptualizing the difference between the perceptual signifier and the linguistic signifier: the thing-presentation and the word-presentation. The thing-presentation is a representation that succeeds in passing itself off as a thing: a representation that masquerades as reality. It is typically specular. Freud tells us that although a thing-presentation consists at least potentially of acoustic, tactile, kinesthetic, and visual elements, complexly interarticulated with each other, it is primarily defined through its visual elements.[1]

As I argued in the previous chapter, although an unconscious memory is capable of manifesting itself as a thing, this capacity remains for the most part latent. As long as it does not succeed in attracting the attention of consciousness to itself, such a memory constitutes only an image-in-potentia. In order to become conscious, and so to become a thing-presentation, it must assume a perceptual form. The thing-presentation would thus finally seem to be Freud's term not for an unconscious memory per se, but rather for what that memory is when it emerges in the form of a perception. The thing-presentation can manifest itself directly, or in the guise of a surrogate. It can also take the form of a hallucination, as it classically does in our dreams, or an external stimulus, as it typically does in waking life.

Although Freud was to elaborate upon the category of the thing-presentation only many years later, his and Breuer's *Studies on Hysteria* provides the paradigmatic text for conceptualizing it, both in its visual qualities and its exteriority. In the opening pages of this text, Freud and Breuer tell us that "*hysterics suffer mainly from reminiscences*" (their emphasis).[2] They seem thereby to define the hysteric as someone more concerned with psychic reality than with the outer world. In the closing pages of *Studies on Hysteria*, though, Freud expresses the view that hysterics are "as a rule of a 'visual' type" (280). The intervening case histories mark the site at which these seemingly divergent claims are mapped on to each other.

The first of the case histories, which is especially important in this respect, tells the story of Anna O., a hysteric who fell ill while nursing her dying father and was subsequently treated by Breuer. Anna O. suffered acutely from reminiscences, but these reminiscences assumed the form of visual perceptions. At times, she experienced "absences," in which she saw not what was actually before her, but rather hallucinations of death's heads and skeletons, along with sundry other things.[3] At other times, rather than replacing the perceptual present, her memories coalesced with it. Her right arm or a bent branch became a snake (38–39), or a brown dress a blue one (33–34). On yet other occasions, her room and everything in it appeared to her not in its contemporary form, but in the guise it had assumed exactly one year before. Breuer had only to hold up an orange before her eyes in order to precipitate the replacement of the present by the past (33). Anna O. seemed to find in this gesture an invitation to exteriorize her mnemonic images—to make of them thing-presentations.

The word-presentation, on the other hand, consists of a linguistic signifier and a linguistic signified. The former is in Freud's account an amalgam of "sound-image," "visual letter-image," "motor speech-image," and "motor writing-image," with the sound image playing the primary role. The latter is a remote derivative of a thing-presentation.[4] I say "remote" because the interarticulation of a thing-presentation with a linguistic signifier radically diminishes its perceptual properties, and hence its affective value. What would otherwise be capable of passing for a thing standing before us is reduced to that vague and generic flash we call a concept.

In appendix C to "The Unconscious," Freud maintains that a word-presentation is "closed." A thing-presentation, on the other hand, is not only "not closed," but cannot in all likelihood be closed (213–14). It is, in fact, as Freud goes on a moment later to emphasize, "open." This distinction is in my view central to a proper understanding of the differences between a word-presentation and a thing-presentation, or—to use language more familiar to my reader—between linguistic signification and perceptual signification.

WORD-PRESENTATION

If we turn to Saussure's *Course in General Linguistics*, a text which is roughly contemporaneous with "The Unconscious," we find ample evidence for Freud's claim that the word-presentation is closed. In this text, Saussure writes that the "linguistic entity is not accurately defined until it is *delimited*, i.e. separated from everything that surrounds it on the phonic chain."[5] This notion of delimitation also appears at every other point in Saussure's account of the linguistic sign. The abstract *langue* or language system is detached from the real; every element within it means not through reference to what resides outside that order, but only through the ways in which it differs from other elements within it (120). A signifier is also properly closed in relation to the signified, and vice-versa; although poetic usage can motivate the relation between the two in all sorts of ways, those signs in which there is no communication between them better exemplify the workings of language than those in which there is (68–69). Finally, although our concrete utterances have the power to work transformatively upon our abstract language system, *parole* is every bit as respectful of the discrete nature of individual words as is *langue*. When we speak "well," we *articulate*: we clearly separate each of our words from those which precede them, and from those which come later (104).

But we need the model of desire which I elaborated in a previous chapter in order to understand what this principle of delimitation really implies. As I indicated there, the wish for perceptual identity is the driving force within psychic life from infancy until death. It is the "agency" behind all forms of signification, whether visual or linguistic. At the beginning of life, as Freud tells us in *The Interpretation of Dreams*, we attempt to achieve perceptual identity through hallucination. Because hallucination is an unsustainable event, it is not long before we turn to the outside world for the satisfaction of our perceptual imperatives. When the sought-after perceptual stimulus fails to arrive, or only partially coincides with our expectations, we are inspired to "think": to mobilize our memories not as an end in and of themselves, but rather as the means to an end.[6]

Thought is an activity which Freud associates with the preconscious: with the psychic locality which intervenes between the unconscious and consciousness, and which—as its name suggests—precedes the latter. In order to think, the preconscious must have unfettered access to the unconscious memories, both individually and as a constellation. It must consequently be able to activate memories without generating either intense pleasure or pain. It must also be able to pursue the connecting ideas between different memories.[7] Neither of these things is possible so long as the unconscious memories retain their original form, since certain of those memories might be said to solicit thought and others to repel it. The relationships between the different images-in-potentia also lack the sensory qualities which would allow them to draw attention to themselves.

These are not the only difficulties in the way of thinking. Although thought is a preconscious activity, we do not conceive of ourselves as thinking until we become conscious of doing so. This is in part because consciousness guards the door leading to what Freud calls "motor response"; because it is only when we become aware of the solution to a particular problem that we are in a position actually to implement that solution. But consciousness is also that toward which preconscious thought tends because "thinking" signifies becoming aware of our thinking process itself.[8] Consciousness, however, is a sensory organ (5: 615), which means that it can only register what is perceptual. Like the relationships between different memories, our thought processes in their primitive form are without sensory qualities.

The preconscious solves all of these problems by "binding" the unconscious memories through language.[9] Binding in part consists of the tying of an almost literal knot: the attachment of a thing-presentation to a linguistic signifier. It makes little difference if we think of this activity as a process to which our unconscious memories must be endlessly subjected, or—as I will be doing here—as one which takes place more or less permanently through their reinscription at the site of the preconscious.[10] In either case, the end result is the same. Attaching linguistic signifiers to our unconscious memories subjugates them. It makes it possible for us to recall them at will; provides the basis for their paradigmatic and syntagmatic organization; and permits us to become aware of our own thought processes.

The binding of a thing-presentation to a linguistic signifier does not seem at first glance suggestive of enclosure. It seems, on the contrary, to open up a whole range of new relationships: the relationship between the thing-presentation and the linguistic signifier; one word-presentation and all of the others; consciousness and the preconscious thought processes; and the preconscious and the connecting paths between our unconscious memories. However, the opening up of all of these relationships is made possible only by the closing down of another—by the inhibition of what might be called "libidinal communication."

The preconscious binds the unconscious memories not merely by attaching linguistic signifiers to them, but also by inhibiting substantial movements of energy between them: by sealing up the pathways along which displacement would otherwise occur.[11] Freud maintains in *Interpretation of Dreams* that the preconscious allows only the small libidinal transfers between thing-presentations which are necessary for thought (5: 599). As a result, a word becomes an isolated cell with its own store of energy. Because this process is repeated with each memory to which a linguistic signifier is bound, the preconscious eventually has at its disposal not merely a collection of individual word-presentations, but a closed system within which energy stagnates.

The advantages of this system are several. In impeding one memory from transferring very much of its libidinal cathexis to another, the preconscious secures the energy it needs for thought. It also prevents one word-presentation from simply taking the place of another, and thereby maintains the distinctions between them. By impeding the impulse toward massive discharge, the preconscious is, in addition, able to bring about and maintain a more or less equal libidinal investment of the mnemonic field.[12] It thereby blocks certain memories from monopolizing consciousness to the exclusion of all others.

However, what represents a gain at the level of rational thought represents a loss at the level of affect. Psychic value is always predicated upon a differential investment—upon the libidinal saturation of certain memories at the expense of others. This is the untranscendable condition of love; there is no democracy within the libidinal domain. The equal investment of the entire field of preconscious memories consequently cannot succeed in making them all important to us; it can only work to eliminate what Saussure calls "positive terms" (120). To seal off the connections linking one word-presentation to another is therefore to shut down our capacity to care.

Finally, the word-presentation closes the door leading to the outside world. As Freud helps us to understand, the only access consciousness has to the outside is through the unconscious;[13] we only know what lies beyond ourselves when perceptions which have been processed elsewhere arrive at consciousness. Since most of what transpires at the level of the unconscious is unavailable to us without language, we necessarily turn to words as an agency for understanding not only internal reality, but also external reality. Unfortunately, though, in the process of making recent or previous perceptual stimuli available to consciousness upon demand, the preconscious cannot help but strip them of their sensory qualities. As a consequence of language, then, our conscious capacity to monitor the psychic domain is increased but our access to the physical domain is radically diminished.

This last point warrants further consideration, since it challenges our usual ways of thinking about the relationship between language and perception. In "The "Unconscious," Freud suggests that a repressed thing-presentation is one to which a linguistic signifier has been denied.[14] He seems thereby to attribute to words the power either to summon forth or to banish unconscious memories. In fact, it would seem that the preconscious thwarts the representational operations of the unconscious more effectively when it *does* provide a verbal linkage than when it *doesn't*, since in the latter case an unconscious memory retains its perceptual potentiality but in the former it loses it. A word-presentation could be said to represent a thing-presentation via negation (*Verneinung*).[15]

Negation is what Freud calls "a substitute, at a higher level, for repression."[16] In negation, "the content of a repressed image or idea can make its way into consciousness, on condition that it is *negated*. Negation is a way of taking cognizance of what is repressed; indeed it is already a lifting of the repression, though not, of course, an acceptance of what is repressed."[17] Freud gives as an example of negation the verbal behavior of an obsessional neurotic, who says to his analyst: "I've got a new obsessive idea . . . and it [occurs] to me . . . that it might mean so and so. But no; that can't be true, or it couldn't have occurred to me."[18]

In this example, Freud's patient effects a linguistic negation of a linguistically organized thought. The implications of this psychic defense for the perceptual signifier are not immediately evident. In *Studies on Hysteria*, however, Freud returns repeatedly to the topic of the relation between the thing-presentation and the word-presentation. And on one occasion, he celebrates the linguistic signifier for its capacity not merely to neutralize the trauma associated with particular memories, but also to divest those memories of their perceptual properties. As soon as a thing-presentation has been "translated" into words, he tells us near the end of that book, it vanishes. It disappears not only for the moment, but forever, apparently losing its capacity even to return in the form of a dream. "When memories return in the form of pictures our task is in general easier than when they return as thoughts," writes Freud, manifesting his usual alertness to the presence of the visual and his insensitivity to its value.

[And] once a picture has emerged from the patient's memory, we may hear from him that it becomes fragmentary and obscure in proportion as he proceeds with his description of it. *The patient is, as it were, getting rid of it by turning it into words.* . . . On . . . occasions . . . a picture of this kind will remain obstinately before the patient's inward eye, in spite of his having described it; and this is an indication to me that he still has something important to tell me about the topic of the picture. As soon as this has been done the picture vanishes, like a ghost that has been laid. (280–81)

THING-PRESENTATION

The thing-presentation is open in all of the ways in which the word-presentation is closed. First of all, except in the case of a simple hallucination, it is always the product of a libidinal transfer either between a perceptual stimulus and at least one memory, or between two or more memories. When we perceive, we do not merely put the perceptual stimulus or substitute memory in the place of the original memory; we also shift at least part of our libidinal cathexis from the latter to the former. It is, indeed, only on the basis of a libidinal transfer that such a replacement can occur. The thing-presentation is itself open to similar communications with subsequent sensory stimuli; with almost any perception, we can— as Freud puts it—"assume the possibility of there being a large number of further impressions in the same chain of associations," impressions which will provide the basis for subsequent displacements.[19] Even after a given perceptual event is ostensibly over, it can continue to assert itself within what we see.

The author of *Interpretation of Dreams* and "The Unconscious" usually refers to the predilection of the unconscious memories for displacement as *mobility*. With the word "mobility," he focuses not upon the memories themselves, but upon the circulation of psychic energy among them. "The cathectic intensities [in the unconscious] are much more mobile," Freud writes in "The Unconscious"; "By the process of *displacement* one idea may surrender its whole quota of cathexis; by the process of *condensation* it may appropriate the whole cathexis of several other ideas" (186). However, as he makes clear in an earlier text, *Project for a Scientific Psychology*, if one unconscious memory can transfer energy to another, this is because the connecting path leading from one to the other is open (298–302).

The thing-presentation is also open to the world. Freud stresses that whereas the preconscious has access to what is outside the psyche only through the unconscious, an access which is not merely indirect, but compromised by the operations of negation, the unconscious is "accessible to the impressions of life."[20] Indeed, "normally all the paths from perception to the *Ucs.* remain open" (194). The unconscious is open to the world because the memories out of which it manufactures perceptions or thing-presentations come into existence only as the result of an encounter between what resides within and what resides without. They might be called "traces" of this encounter.

Finally, the thing-presentation has the potential to effect in the one who sees it an affective opening-up. Freud defines it in "The Unconscious" as "the first and true object-cathex[is]" (201), thereby suggesting that it is not only how we first reach out to others, but how we continue to do so. In addition to representing our primary affective way of communicating with other creatures and things, a thing-presentation can extend our capacity to care in new directions. Each time we allow an unconscious memory to assume a different form, we expand the field of things that can be important to us.

Freud maintains that the flow of unconscious libido through the field of memories creates a *Bahnung*. This noun, which Strachey infelicitously translates as "facilitation," means "the blazing or pushing through of a path." It is thus a word suggestive of something which is underway, but not yet completed: of a process which is very much "in progress." Freud first deploys this word in *Project for a Scientific Psychology*, where he uses it to talk about the wearing down of the barriers separating unconscious memories or "neurones" from each other.[21] In subsequent texts, Freud conceives of the *Bahnung* less mechanistically: in *Interpretation of Dreams* and *The Psychopathology of Everyday Life*, the links connecting one memory to another are not neurological, but rather associational. Whether conceived literally or metaphorically, though, the *Bahnung* or preferred pathway constitutes the itinerary of desire. It determines not only the directions in which libido can flow—which unconscious memories will be revisited each time, and in which order—but where it is possible for each of us to "go," affectively speaking.

We should not construe this determination too narrowly, however; the *Bahnung* is writ in time, not stone. With our perceptual speech we are constantly remaking the path along which our desire is destined to move, and that will be true until the moment of death. Each new perceptual stimulus that is incorporated into the *Bahnung*, through its associative links to what has come before, has the potential to extend it, sometimes in a different direction. Moreover, although the resulting thing-presentation derives its meaning through reference back to what precedes it, it also possesses the capacity to act transformatively on the past.

This is because, as Freud suggests in an important passage from *Studies in Hysteria*, the *Bahnung* or pathway of unconscious desire does not pursue a straight line; rather, it loops back to earlier moments; branches off laterally, creating side roads off the main road; and produces what might be called "traffic circles," from which a whole concatenation of new paths can be reached. Freud compares the itinerary followed by displacement first to a line which has passed along "the most roundabout paths from the surface [memories] to the deepest layers and back"; then to the zig-zag patterns of the knight's move in chess; and finally to a "ramifying system of lines and more particularly to a converging one" (289–90).[22]

Each subject's *Bahnung* traces something like an affective Milky Way across the sky of his past. But even within this celestial constellation, which stands out against the somber background of less important memories, certain stars shine more brightly than others. These stars also cast an unusually wide circle of illumination. They consequently light the way to more new libidinal territories than other stars. They also illuminate more old ones, sometimes even transforming what was once a nocturnal desert into a garden of earthly delights.

I began talking about the thing-presentation as if it were an articulatable unit, like the word-presentation. It should be evident by now that this is not in fact the case. Since the thing-presentation means only through reference back to what it in turn helps to transform, it cannot be isolated from the *Bahnung* without losing its status as signifier. It is part of a constantly changing continuum. In *Studies in Hysteria*, Freud describes the memories which make up the *Bahnung* as a "spatially-extended mass" (291). He also explains that our impression of those memories as discrete units derives from the fact that it is only by being cut up that this mass can become available to consciousness. Consciousness is like the proverbial eye of the needle, through which the camel of the *Bahnung* cannot pass. Only by being disassembled into discrete units, and attached to linguistic signifiers, can the constellation of unconscious memories finally make its way through that narrow pass. "There is some justification for speaking of the 'defile' of consciousness," Freud begins:

Only a single memory at a time can enter ego-consciousness. A patient who is occupied in working through such a memory sees nothing of what is pushing after it and forgets what has already pushed its way through. If there are difficulties in the way of mastering this single pathogenic memory . . . then the defile is, so to speak, blocked. The work is at a stand-still, nothing more can appear, and the single memory which is in process of breaking through remains in front of the patient until he has taken it up into the breadth of his ego. The whole spatially-extended mass of psychogenic material is in this way drawn through a narrow cleft and thus arrives in consciousness cut up, as it were, into pieces or strips. (291)

THE INAUGURATION OF DESIRE

None of us is perceptually open in all the ways I have just described at the moment of birth. Like all languages, the language of our desire is something into which we must be inducted. Freud's theory of the drive can provide us with a partial model for conceptualizing how we come to be the speakers of this predominantly visual language. The drive, Freud explains in "Instincts and Their Vicissitudes," is a borderline entity, one located on the "frontier between the mental and the somatic."[23] It consists on the one hand of an ideational representative, and on the other of a stimulus "originating from within the organism and reaching the mind, as a measure of the demand made upon the mind for work in consequence of its connection with the body" (122). The ideational representative is a thing-presentation, but one which has been alienated from itself. This particular thing-presentation is no longer simply a memory capable of assuming a perceptual form, but a delegate for something which itself exceeds representation.

The ideational representative of a drive can be repressed. The stimulus of the drive, however, cannot.[24] It continues agitating for perceptual representation even after its ideational representative has been denied access to consciousness. This agitation is productive of what we think of as "psychic energy," "libido," or "excitement." It also precipitates a potentially infinite series of libidinal displacements onto substitute ideational representatives. The memories and perceptual stimuli through which the drive seeks substitute fulfillment may succeed in reaching consciousness. However, if their connection to the repressed ideational representative becomes too evident, they, too, are likely to be repressed.

In "Repression," Freud distinguishes between what he calls "primal repression" and all subsequent repressions, which he characterizes as "secondary repression" (148). When an ideational representative undergoes secondary repression, it is both pushed out of the preconscious and drawn toward the unconscious. Secondary repression is to be distinguished in this last respect from primal repression, which involves only the first of these operations. In primal repression, Freud explains, the ideational representative of the drive is refused admission to the preconscious but there is no corresponding attraction exercised by the unconscious. This is because there is as yet no unconscious. It is only around the first ideational representative that the unconscious can form.

Before primal repression, the relationship between a particular ideational representative and its somatic force is apparently provisional. However, when an ideational representative is primally repressed, the connection between it and the somatic force of the drive becomes permanent.[25] Freud refers to the relationship which is thereby established as a "fixation." Fixation is a concept which usually has a negative meaning in psychoanalysis. In "Instincts and Their Vicissitudes," for instance, Freud says that it "puts an end to [the] mobility [of the drive] through its intense opposition to detachment" (123). However, it seems that a permanent attachment of the drive to this particular ideational representative is in fact liberating rather than arresting. Rather than precluding displacement, it enables it.

Freud writes that the primally repressed term functions as a magnet, drawing other material into the unconscious. It does so in order to make possible those libidinal transfers between itself and other memories which will result in the ultimate emergence of a surrogate thing-presentation. Freud writes in "Repression" that this ideational representative attracts "everything with which it can establish a connection" (148). He makes the same point even more forcefully on the next page: we "forget too readily that repression does not hinder the instinctual representative from continuing to exist in the unconscious, from organizing itself further, putting out derivatives and establishing connections" (149).

Fixation is not only something which occurs as a result of repression; it is itself the mechanism through which repression occurs. This is because it is by establishing a *preconscious fixation* that the psyche brings about an *unconscious fixation*. Here, however, "fixation" signifies not only a libidinal, but also a topographical arrestation. Displacement is also not that to which fixation mysteriously gives rise, but a virtual synonym for it. The primally repressed term, we learn in "The Unconscious," is excluded from its position as the potentially conscious ideational representative of the drive-force by putting a second term in its place. The substitutory ideational representative is then secured in its protective position through a series of further displacements.

Freud explains the defensive uses to which libidinal transfer can be put through a curious metaphor. He suggests that the second ideational representative prevents the first from reentering the preconscious by surrounding itself with a "protective wall."[26] It builds this protective wall by annexing a circle of affiliated memories—by seeking out the same kinds of connections about which Freud speaks in his discussion of primal repression. This circle of affiliated memories must be expanded each time the first ideational representative tries to reclaim its position. Freud refers to the topographical arrestation of an ideational representative through displacement as an *anticathexis*.[27]

'DAS DING'

In Freud's account of repression, we find a peculiar mirroring at the preconscious level of what happens at the unconscious level: in both cases, we find the paradoxical combination of a libidinal fixation and a proclivity for displacement. However, it is only in the case of secondary repression that Freud makes displacement the agency of libidinal fixation. It is also only in the case of secondary repression that Freud conceives of fixation topographically—as the arrestation of an ideational representative in a defensive position.

In my view, however, the primally repressed term performs a similar function in every respect to that which replaces it. It, too, is subject to a topographical fixation; it, too, that is, works to exclude and continue excluding something by occupying the place which the latter would otherwise fill. The defensive role which it performs, moreover, is even more crucial than that performed by its preconscious counterpart. What the topographical arrestation of the first unconscious thing-presentation defends us against is not simply a forbidden perception, but rather the end of desire. This is because, in remaining in the position into which it has been inserted, the primally repressed term blocks the reentrance into the psyche of what Lacan variously calls "being," "presence," or *das Ding*. Finally, like the term which displaces it in the preconscious, the primally repressed term is secured in its protective position through a host of subsequent displacements, which might be said not only to encircle it, but also to raise or elevate it.

We are obliged to posit an unconscious as well as a preconscious anticathexis because the story of subjectivity does not begin in quite the way Freud suggests in the metapsychological papers,[28] with the psychic representation of a somatic force. Rather, it begins with the predominantly visual drive toward perceptual identity. There is initially no ideational representative as such, and no somatic drive-force, only a thing-presentation toward whose perceptual realization the psyche moves. The thing-presentation is also at this juncture more or less interchangeable with a range of other thing-presentations. At a certain point, however, the drive toward perceptual identity comes up against the force of repression in its attempt to revive the thing-presentation, and it becomes fixated to it.

The process whereby the prohibited thing-presentation is relegated to the unconscious occurs just as Freud suggests, through a preconscious anticathexis. This anticathexis is, however, more than a defensive maneuver against the perceptual realization of a particular thing-presentation. It is also the means by which at least two thing-presentations are alienated from themselves. When one thing-presentation takes the place of another as its preconscious representative, it ceases to be simply a potentially perceptual memory; it becomes as well a signifier for what it has replaced. This substitutory thing-presentation also obliges what it represses to function as its signified.[29] Henceforth, no perceptual event will ever again be identical with itself. Every perceptual stimulus or memory will always function as a signifier of a prior one.

With the constitution of one thing-presentation as a signifier, and another as its signified, a second exclusion is effected—this time not simply from the preconscious, but from the psyche *tout court.* "Being" evaporates, leaving behind a void or lack. Now at last the primally repressed thing-presentation becomes what Freud says it is, an "ideational representative." However, what it stands in for psychically is not a somatic drive force, but rather the "here and now."

Lacan maintains in *Seminar VII* that it is at the moment that one thing-presentation pushes another into the unconscious that the subject enters language, and not through the production of two linguistically opposed sounds.[30] This is a crucial modification of his own theory, and one with which I am in fundamental agreement. The thing-presentation comes first, and subsequently provides the word-presentation with its signified. It is also by means of the thing-presentation rather than the word-presentation that the subject performs its first libidinal speech act. Very early in the subject's life the primally repressed thing-presentation begins to function not merely as a signified to another thing-presentation, but also as a surrogate for "being"—as the first and most important of the many terms which will symbolize what has been lost through the entry into language. The primally repressed thing-presentation thus paradoxically comes to embody what it also excludes.

UNCONSCIOUS ANTICATHEXIS

Freud connects anticathexis to an increase in excitation both in "The Unconscious" and *Beyond the Pleasure Principle.*[31] However, he elaborates the connection between anticathexis and excitation very differently in these two texts. In *Beyond the Pleasure Principle,* anticathexis constitutes a kind of energic "crisis management." Through it, the psyche seeks to reduce the excitation which can originate from an alien stimulus to a constant level. It does so by binding the excitatory stimulus linguistically, and by dispersing the excitation which it has generated in the psyche evenly over a circumscribed field of memories (30–35). Although "dispersal" is here another word for "displacement," the kinds of displacements through which this state of constancy is achieved are presumably not the large ones which Freud associates with libidinal investment, but rather the small ones necessary for thought. In "The Unconscious," on the other hand, Freud maintains that an anticathexis results in a heightening of excitation. He also suggests that the "whole of the associated environment of the substitutive idea" is "cathected with special intensity" (183). He thereby indicates that the displacements through which an anticathexis is created involve substantial libidinal transfers. These are not simple argumentative discrepancies. Freud is speaking about preconscious anticathexis in *Beyond the Pleasure Principle*. In "The Unconscious," on the other hand, he is unwittingly describing the kind of anticathexis through which *das Ding* is excluded from the psyche.

It might seem odd that, after emphasizing the similarities between the preconscious and the unconscious anticathexes, I should now insist upon their difference. However, although the preconscious and unconscious anticathexes might both be said to serve a defensive function, and to do so through establishing relations with other memories, the latter obeys a different energic logic than the former. The preconscious anticathexis attempts to reduce the excitation precipitated in it by an alien stimulus by connecting thing-presentations to word-presentations, and through effecting the kind of microdisplacements which are specific to linguistically organized thought. The unconscious anticathexis, on the other hand, itself *creates* psychic excitation. The "fading"[32] of "being" results in an insatiable psyche, and so a permanent source of drive energy. As long as the unconscious anticathexis is in place, moreover, not even the preconscious can achieve real constancy; the psyche is constantly "charged" anew. The unconscious anticathexis also does not respond to excitation by attempting to "bind" it. Rather—as I suggested in the previous chapter—it typically converts quantity into quality. Displacement provides the agency of this conversion.

Since we generally conceptualize displacement as the removal of a libidinal cathexis from one thing so as to invest it in another, it is not easy to see how it could result in a qualitative complexification; to displace away from something seems, on the contrary, to abandon it. I would like to suggest, however, that transferring libido from one term to another can also provide a means of elevating the first term: of "raising" it, as Lacan would say, to the "dignity" of *das Ding*.[33] We elevate or ennoble something through displacement when we displace not away from it, but "around" it—when we connect it to a host of related memories and thereby expand its field of meaning.

In *Seminar VII*, Lacan describes the modus operandi of this sort of displacement. He, too, attributes it to a surplus of excitation. "When the usual limit of psychic energy is exceeded," Lacan explains, it "is scattered and diffused within the psychic organism; the quantity is transformed into complexity. In a kind of expansion of the lighted zone of the neuronic [or mnemonic] organism, here and there in the distance, it lights up according to the laws of associative facilitation, or constellations of *Vorstellungen* which regulate the association of ideas, unconscious *Gedanken*, according to the pleasure principle" (58–59).[34]

But what produces the heightened excitement through which certain memories come to be privileged over others? Freud makes the fascinating observation in *Beyond the Pleasure Principle* that it is because of a constant influx of difference that living organisms do not die as soon as they are born. This influx of difference is life-sustaining, because it is productive of psychic excitation. Death can come only when excitation is reduced to a zero degree.[35] He thereby establishes a close correlation between difference and excitation.

I would like to use this passage from *Beyond the Pleasure Principle* as the inspiration for an equally speculative claim: The kind of displacement through which one displaces "around" something, rather than away from it, producing what might be characterized as "megastars" in the Milky Way of the *Bahnung*, occurs when we succeed not only in seeing once again in it what we most yearn to see, but in registering the differences which distinguish that thing from what it represents. Our excitation is at such times unusually high because we are stimulated from two different directions: from the direction of the psyche itself and from the direction of the world. Although the apprehension of an object's difference can take an infinitude of forms, it is almost always with the registration of that object's visual particularity that it begins.

THE NONREPRESENTATIVE REPRESENTATIVE

It is presumably because of the closed nature of the linguistic signifier that Lacan usually attributes to it rather than the perceptual signifier the role of inducing the "fading" of "being." The linguistic signifier is at its most definitive a *nonrepresentative representation*, one whose relation both to its signified and its referent is purely arbitrary.[36] The perceptual signifier, on the other hand, is conventionally *representative*; when it replaces another signifier or coalesces with it, that is generally on the basis of a similarity or a contiguity. It might therefore seem difficult to understand how the visual signifier can induce the "fading" of "being."

However, unlike all subsequent acts of perceptual signification, the one by means of which lack is installed in the psyche is not motivated by formal affinities. On the contrary, the originary ideational representative provides a completely unmotivated stand-in for what it represents. This is in part because "being" is devoid of qualities. It is not a love-object, but rather the impossible nonobject of desire. Only by virtue of its retroactive symbolization will it be given lineaments and a face.[37] But it is also because primal repression itself creates the sole criterion upon which the first ideational representative assumes its substitutory role; it is only by virtue of being "barred" or "excluded" that it can become a delegate for "being." Since no intrinsic attribute prepares it for the role it plays, the first ideational representative could at least hypothetically be replaced by any other ideational representative.[38] The motivated relationships between one ideational representation and another which subsequently come into play do so only on the basis of this originating arbitrariness.

The first ideational representative of "being" is the site of a traumatic nonmeaning.[39] The word "traumatic" carries here precisely the value Freud attributes to it in *Beyond the Pleasure Principle*: it means "conducive of a state of radical excitation." The primally repressed term precipitates a dangerously high state of psychic excitement because it is difference personified. It introduces division and delay into a psyche which has previously known only the "here and now." The primally repressed thing-presentation is also the *first* ideational representative. There is consequently no prior term to which to refer it and through which to make it meaningful and familiar. It remains an opaque and alien intruder. At the same time, this stranger makes a powerful affective claim upon the subject whose psyche it enters; although its intrusion into the unconscious precipitates the "fading" of "being," it provides a stand-in for what has been lost. There is clearly enough excitement here to last a lifetime.

But this is not to say that we will never again encounter anything as exciting as the object represented by the first ideational representative. The primally repressed term does not function like a Platonic Idea; it is not the prototype from which all necessarily inferior copies derive. It is, rather, entirely dependent upon what comes later for its meaning. Isolated from what replaces it, every subject's first ideational representative would be as nonsensical as the word *fort* the first time Freud's grandson uttered it.[40]

THE MATERNAL METAPHOR

I have spoken at various moments in the preceding discussion of repression as if the process whereby a perceptual memory comes to be installed as the first representative of *das Ding* were somehow autonomous—as if repression "performed" itself. In fact, of course, primal repression is a family matter. It generally occurs in our culture through the Oedipus complex. And, although the mother and the father are themselves always unconsciously responding to the prior dictates of a particular kinship structure in doing so, it is generally they who take it upon themselves first to precipitate and then to prohibit the desires which are specific to that complex.

As every reader of "On a Question Preliminary to Any Possible Treatment of Psychosis" or *Seminar III* knows, repression is for Lacan virtually synonymous with the normative or heterosexual Oedipus complex.[41] It also brings about what he calls the "paternal metaphor." As a result of the mother's desire for the father, the phallus comes to be inscribed below the bar of repression as a privileged representative of "being." However, Lacan often stresses the maternal nature of the first term through which the subject metaphorizes *das Ding* in *Seminar VII*,[42] and in his seminar on *Hamlet* he attests to the difficulty of getting beyond this originary signifier of loss to the phallus.[43] This is in my view because that latter term does not often enjoy the privileged value which Lacan attributes to it.

As I have already suggested in previous chapters, a kinship structure finally consists of nothing more than an incest taboo. This enabling prohibition, which can assume many different forms, imposes itself most forcefully in our culture at the site of the primary caretaker. Since the mother still conventionally performs that role in our culture, it is classically through the denial of perceptual form to a libidinally charged memory of her that the subject enters kinship—through what might be called the "maternal metaphor."

Even after the subject has acceded to the signifier, the mother must remain in her originary position. She cannot be removed from her privileged place because she is the barrier blocking the backward path leading to a full and complete satisfaction; because she is the finger in the dike preventing the psyche from being inundated with presence; because without her there can be neither signifier nor the passion of the signifier. However, once the maternal metaphor has taken place, the mother represents as impossible an object of desire as *das Ding*. Only so long as she is excluded from consciousness can she function both as the signified to which all other signifiers refer, and as the primary representative of "being." She cannot, therefore, be perceptually revived without losing her privileged status. The mother also performs her crucial functions only as a result of our constant displacements away from her. Finally, it is these displacements themselves which determine what "mother" can mean. Consequently, in spite of all of the social and ideological encroachments that work to impose retroactive restrictions upon her, our originary love-object may be the closest any of us ever comes to pure limitlessness. It is through loving the mother that we are able to love the world.

SHOWING SAYING

As has no doubt been evident all along, the thing-presentation and the word-presentation do not always remain where they "belong." The preconscious helps to determine which thing-presentation shall be pushed first below the bar of repression and thereby eternalized as the primary signifier of desire. Language also plays an important subsequent role in helping to determine what psychic elements are enlisted as secondary representatives of *das Ding*. And many elements of the unconscious belong systemically to the preconscious, in that they are verbally organized and "free from self-contradiction."[44] As Lacan says, "the things of the human world are things in a universe structured by words . . . language, symbolic processes, dominate and govern all."[45]

But if the perceptual signifier can tilt in the direction of the verbal signifier, the verbal signifier can also mutate in the direction of the perceptual signifier. Freud tells us in "The Unconscious" that a large part of the preconscious retains "the character of its [unconscious] derivatives" (191). This means not merely that some preconscious elements remain in close communication with what is repressed, but also that others retreat from or refuse to succumb to rationalization.

Word-presentations are consequently not always closed. There are times when they are ordered less according to paradigmatic and syntagmatic rules than according to the libidinal principles of the thing-presentation. At such times, they stop functioning as the agency whereby unconscious processes are negated, and become carriers of unconscious desire. The verbal field ceases to be governed by the principle of *Gleichbesetzung*[46] or "equal investment." Instead, libido is freely displaced from one similar or contiguous term to another, until a rich and affectively charged associational network has been created.

Unconscious desire acts as a constant prompt on preconscious thought not merely to give voice to unconscious memory, but also to do so in a visual form. Words find this appeal enormously seductive. As we have seen, Freud speaks in *Interpretation of Dreams* about the attraction exercised by the potentially "visual memories in the unconscious" on the preconscious thoughts (5: 596). He also refers in "The Metapsychology of Dreams" to the appeal which visual memories exercise over "thoughts which have been put into words."[47] Words, it seems, can never entirely transcend their origin in perception.[48]

In our dreams, our verbal thoughts generally succumb to the attraction of our potentially visual memories so completely that they, too, assume a visual form. There is at such moments a seamless join of the past and the present: an old affect finds a new residence, but gives no sign that it has ever resided anywhere else. The memory of the book of colored plates Freud and his sister tore apart as children coalesces with the memory of the illustrated monographs he bought as a medical student and the one he recently saw in a shop window to represent a published copy of *Interpretation of Dreams*.[49] The spectacle of one woman's oral cavity is made to stand simultaneously for the unpleasing dentures earlier seen in the mouth of another woman and for a hoped-for view of a very different female opening.[50]

In our waking lives, however, there is seldom such an absolute conflation of two memories with each other, or of a memory with a perceptual stimulus. Even when we stop using language in the mode of negation, and begin using it instead to represent representationally what we have seen or desire to see, our words cannot help but maintain some distance between the terms which unconscious desire seeks to unify. Instead of asserting the equivalence of two heterogeneous things, or even condensing a whole associational network of memories into a single term, we generate metaphors and metonymies, tropes in which there is a constant libidinal coming and going between representation and what is represented.

At such times, we do not so much look in the mode of showing as *show* our look. For the most part, there is no spectator to receive what we display. However, when we address our showing saying either to the symbolic Other, or to others as such, they are able to see not only *what* we see but *how* we see. In so doing, they provide us with something no dream can ever give us: the perspective from which we, too, can look at our look. Showing saying is thus finally as disclosive of the specificity of our particular perceptual passion as it is of the world.

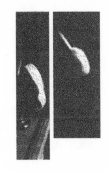

6

THE LANGUAGE OF THINGS

Nature is a temple, where the living
Columns sometimes breathe confusing speech;
Man walks within these graves of symbols, each
Of which regards him as a kindred thing.

As the long echoes, shadowy, profound,
Heard from afar, blend into a unity,
Vast as the night, as sunlight's clarity,
So perfumes, colors, sounds may correspond.

Odors there are, fresh as a baby's skin,
Mellow as oboes, green as meadow grass,
—Others corrupted, rich, triumphant, full,

Having dimensions infinitely vast,
Frankincense, musk, ambergris, benjamin,
Singing the senses' rapture, and the soul's.
—Charles Baudelaire, "Correspondences,"
    translated by James McGowan

We have traveled a long way since the beginning of this book.
We have abandoned our rarefied place in the sun of a single and

nonsensuous Good and descended into the domain where beauty is multiple, although still nonsensuous. From there, we have climbed down into the thick atmosphere of the cave, domain of firelight and shadows. With great effort, we have also found our way back to that place which is our place, the one from which it is possible to see what is given to us alone to see. Finally, we have acknowledged the presence of those sitting around us, and are ready to begin listening to their language and speaking our own. We have become again what we were before the birth of metaphysics: world spectators. However, something crucial is still missing: those already existing creatures and things which the God of Genesis brought before Adam to be named.[1] Unless they join us, we cannot see and the world cannot appear.

It might not seem possible for the animals and birds to come before us, one by one. Is not what Plato represents as the cave of the world really a prison house of signs? Are we not doomed when attempting to apprehend things in themselves to see precisely what the father of philosophy tells us that the cave dwellers see: shadows of simulacra, copies of copies? In fact, although I have consistently associated the kind of signification which I have privileged here with the sublation of creatures and things out of the real and into a "more-than-real," I do not believe that we inhabit a prison house of signs.

If words represented our only form of symbolization, we would indeed be hopelessly estranged from the world. Not only would we be unable to determine with any assurance whether anything else existed, we would also remain forever in irresolute doubt as to whether we ourselves did. Like Descartes, we would be obliged to verify our reality exclusively by means of our capacity to think.[2] However, words do not constitute our only or even our primary means of symbolization. Visual perception comes first, and visual perception is not located "in" us. It is situated, rather, at the point at which memory meets external stimulus.

To look, it is not enough to contemplate the "supersensible substrate" of an object.[3] There must be what Freud calls "perceptual identity,"[4] or Heidegger the "presencing" of the look towards what is present.[5] Something must give itself to be seen, and a spectator must see within it the miraculous reincarnation of the what-has-been. It is, moreover, not the perceiving subject, but rather the perceptual object which plays the initiating role in this scopic transaction. The world "intends"[6] toward being seen; it aspires or moves toward appearance. When we look at other creatures and things in the way that I described in the last two chapters, it is also in response to their very precise solicitation to us to do so.

INTENDING OBJECTS

In imputing an intentionality to the world to appear, I am drawing in part upon Hannah Arendt's account of appearance in *The Life of the Mind.* In the section of that text entitled "The World's Phenomenal Nature," she suggests that there is something like a reversibility to the categories of seeing and being seen. Every perceiving subject is at moments a perceptual object, and every perceptual object at times a perceiving subject.[7] This is an argument which both Merleau-Ponty and Lacan made before her,[8] with the primary purpose of demonstrating the interiority of the perceiving subject to the field of vision. Arendt, however, is less concerned with demonstrating that no one and nothing can escape visibility than with establishing the absolute priority within the field of vision of the aspiration to be seen. "*Whatever can see wants to be seen,*" she writes, "*whatever can hear calls out to be heard, whatever can touch presents itself to be touched*" (29; her emphasis). As Arendt herself suggests later in *The Life of the Mind,* the ubiquity of this aspiration obliges us to impute to objects as well as to subjects something like an intentionality to be seen: "All objects because they appear indicate a subject, and, just as every subjective act has its intentional object, so every appearing object has its intentional subject" (46).

Whether we locate intentionality at the site of consciousness, the unconscious, or language, we are accustomed to thinking of it as something specific to the human psyche. The category of an "intending object" is consequently one to which we are likely to accede only so long as it designates a human being. However, early in *The Life of the Mind* Arendt makes clear that this category is at least for her all-inclusive, one which includes even inanimate, dead, and man-made substances. She also encourages us to locate intentionality in a very surprising place: in what might be called "brute materiality." "Dead matter, natural and artificial, changing and unchanging, depends in its being, that is, in its appearingness, on the presence of living creatures," she asserts; "Nothing and nobody exists in this world whose very being does not presuppose a *spectator*. . . . everything that is is meant to be perceived by somebody" (19).

Arendt draws extensively in this section of *The Life of the Mind* upon the work of the Austrian biologist and zoologist Adolf Portmann. In his extraordinary book *Animal Forms and Patterns: A Study of the Appearance of Animals*, Portmann offers an intransigently antifunctionalist account of animal appearance. He argues against the prevalent notion that the colors, forms, or marking of a bird's plumage or an animal's fur are motivated by the demands of self-preservation or are a simple outgrowth of internal activities.[9] Portmann maintains instead that we are presented in all such cases with "optical structures, organs to be looked at." These structures and organs, moreover, achieve their full meaning only when they are in fact apprehended by a "beholding eye" (111–12).

It is not merely the so-called "higher" animal forms which in Portmann's view intend toward being seen. The author of *Animal Forms and Patterns* also makes this claim with respect to animal forms which are hardly even sentient. Indeed, he points out several times that the "lower type[s] of animal life," in which "the individual inner life of experience is but poorly developed," are often the richest in their "wealth of forms" (196–97). This obliges Portmann to sheer off intentionality altogether from the psyche, and to account for it in radically revisionary ways.

Portmann has repeated recourse to passive constructions when describing the surfacing of an aspiration to be seen within the natural world, suggesting that self-showing is there an action without an actant, at least in the conventional sense of the word. Animal forms and patterns are "directed toward a beholding eye," he writes in the passage from which I quoted in the preceding paragraph. They are "designed in a very special way to meet the eye of the beholder," he insists in another (25). "The forms surrounding us are not utterly haphazard, but 'compositions' which are being performed," he claims in yet another passage, now overtly defining self-display as an event devoid of an agent (162). Intentionality finally emerges as an actional "tending toward," whose origin can be no more biologically than psychically localized.

Although this intention is—according to Arendt—inherent in matter itself, it is apparently capable of giving rise to forms as complex and elaborate as the most subjectively driven visual display. Portmann repeatedly proposes that the principles which hold sway within animal appearance are analogous to those classically governing aesthetic production (11, 22, 23–24, and 107): symmetry, harmony, the subordination of the part to the whole, and the value of surface beauty for its own sake. He also suggests that animal patterns and forms make demands upon us equal to those of a theatrical production (161–62).

Roger Caillois, the French philosopher and one-time surrealist, reaches similar conclusions to Portmann's in a series of texts devoted to the visual forms assumed by insects and semiprecious stones.[10] He, too, stresses that these forms serve no self-preservative function, even in those cases where insects engage in what has been traditionally assumed to be protective coloration. He, too, suggests that when nonhuman creatures make themselves visible or invisible, it is strictly for the sake of visibility or invisibility; indeed, he suggests that self-showing, or what he calls "an ostentatious outpouring of resources" may be "a wider and more [obeyed] law than the strict vital interest, the imperative of the survival of the species."[11]

Finally, Caillois too proposes that some kind of aesthetic drive is implicit within the forms and patterns assumed by insects and rocks, and compares its results to artistic production. "[T]here appears to be an autonomous aesthetic force in the world of biology in general," he maintains at one point in *The Mask of Medusa* (41). In another passage from the same text, he does more than compare nature's products once again to art. He also compares nature to an artist. "Rocks, too, supply natural works of art that have such a resemblance to paintings and have so struck the imagination of observers that at times they have been led to think of nature herself as [a kind of] artist," he writes in the passage in question (43).

One of the most fascinating parts of Caillois's discussion of rock forms and patterns is his account of the nineteenth-century Chinese practice of framing pieces of marble, as if they were actual works of art, and adding the signature of the framer to them.[12] Here, the human artist might be said to subjectivize the objective intention which made itself so strongly felt at the moment of discovery. Caillois, himself, does much the same thing through the title which he gives his study of rocks: *The Writing of Stones*.

But Arendt's emphasis on matter cannot finally be reconciled with Caillois's and Portmann's on form in the way I suggested a few pages ago. Form is not the agency whereby matter communicates to us its prior intention to appear. Rather, a creature or thing's form is indistinguishable from its aspiration to be seen. It is also at the site of its formal parameters that this creature or thing realizes or fails to realize its Being. Appearance is a definitionally aesthetic event: the bringing forward, into the light of visibility, of a unique constellation of formal coordinates.

INTENDED SUBJECTS

As I have argued at length in the last two chapters, it is we alone who provide the light by means of which creatures and things appear. We illuminate the world by affirming it in its visual specificity. I would now like to advance the philosophically unthinkable addendum to this claim: the stripes on the Bengal tiger, the peeling of the bark of the eucalyptus tree, and the ruffles on the top of the New England daffodil themselves solicit this affirmation. The world does not simply give itself to be seen; it gives itself to be loved.

Astonishing as this claim might seem to be, I am not alone in making it. Both Caillois and Portmann come close to suggesting that the eye by means of which stones, insects, and animals aim to be seen is a human eye. In characterizing rock patterns and forms at one point as a kind of signification, and at other points as a form of aesthetic production, Caillois intimates that we are ourselves their point of address. And, at the same time that Portmann, like Arendt, denies the intrinsic connection between intentionality and humanness, he makes clear that without subjectivity the end to-ward which animal patterns and forms aim cannot be realized. In one passage, he indicates that the eye through which animals seek to be seen is that either of a member of the same species or an enemy (111–12). However, for the most part he maintains that we are the spectator to whom this appeal is made. This is because what animal forms and patterns incline toward is affective affirmation. An animal's coat or a bird's plumage has as its aim the "rais[ing of] its wearer to a place apart," Portmann claims at one point (25). The bodily forms of such creatures are "part of the way in which the special quality of the high-ranking animal form is represented," he says at another; "they belong to the many organs through which a high-ranking organism expresses its intrinsic worth" (182).

The world becomes beautiful or wonderful only when we sculpt our void in its image. In attempting to express what Portmann calls its "intrinsic worth," the world could consequently be said to call for what has been so often defined in opposition to it—human desire. It could indeed be said to "want" the human psyche, in all of its psychoanalytic specificity. If, as phenomenology teaches us, the subject tends toward objects, the reverse is then apparently equally true. Our subjectivity is objectively intended.

BEINGS WHO LACK BEING

It is not merely that our subjectivity is objectively intended. It is also that we ourselves are intending objects as well as desiring subjects. By this I do not mean merely that, in addition to seeing, we wish to be seen; rather, I mean that we tend toward appearance in the same a-subjective sense in which rocks or insects do. Here I find myself arguing not so much with as against Roger Caillois, as well as with his most important commentator, Lacan.

In *The Mask of Medusa*, Caillois emphasizes what might be called the "existential" nature of nature's aesthetic production, and distinguishes it from human art. "[T]he wing," he writes, "is part of the butterfly[,] whereas the artist invents and carries out his picture himself" (31). Even when insects are capable of assuming a second form, the result is—as Caillois puts it—"a photography on the level of the object and not on that of the image, a reproduction in three-dimensional space with solids and [depth]: sculpture-photography or better *teleplasty*."[13] Since it is through its being that an insect contributes to the aesthetic domain, it also has at its disposal a much narrower range of expressive means than the human artist.

Although opposing human and insect mimicry on the basis of the aesthetic nature of the former and the existential basis of the latter, Caillois nevertheless uses human mimicry as the paradigm for interpreting insect mimicry. When a butterfly transforms itself into a leaf or another insect, he tells us, that is a "pure disguise," a departure from its true being. Morphological metamorphoses within the domain of insects can consequently be compared to fashion within the domain of humans; they constitute the assumption of something inauthentic or inessential.[14] To argue both that insect mimicry is existential and a fashion or disguise, as Caillois does, is to suggest that certain natural creatures are inauthentic in their very being. The masks worn by the human subject, on the other hand, can be donned and doffed; they seemingly do not encroach upon that subject's being.

In *Four Fundamental Concepts of Psycho-Analysis*, Lacan modifies Caillois's paradigm in certain key ways.[15] He maintains that when a nonhuman creature assumes another form, that form is as extrinsic to its being as it is in the case of the subject. Such an entity consequently cannot be said to be deceptive in its essence. But if nonhuman creatures resemble the subject in their capacity to break up into "semblance" and "being" (107), the subject also resembles nonhuman creatures in a number of respects. First, like the insects described by Caillois, the subject might be said to solicit an external agency. This agency, which Lacan calls the "gaze,"[16] represents something like "Otherness" within the field of vision; it is consequently structural rather than human. The subject solicits the gaze because she depends upon it for her visibility. She effects this solicitation in much the way Caillois's insects do: by assuming an extrinsic form. This is because there is no unmediated visibility; the gaze always *"photo-graph[s]"* or ratifies what it apprehends in the guise of an intervening image or "screen" (106; his emphasis).

For Lacan, the distinguishing feature of human subjectivity is not authenticity, as Caillois seems perversely to argue, but rather knowledge. Insects and animals, he maintains, cannot distinguish the masks they assume from themselves; they are consequently "captured" by the form in whose guise they are apprehended.[17] The subject, on the other hand, knows—or at least *can know*—that she is always seen through a representational "grid." She is therefore in a position to do something which the insect cannot do: she can "play" with the image which defines her.[18]

Although the modifications to which Lacan subjects Caillois's account of mimicry make it rich in implications for our understanding of sexual, racial, and economic difference, it is no more adequate to the task of theorizing appearance than the text upon which it draws. When an insect or animal assumes another bodily form, it does not either falsify or depart from its essence. Rather, it becomes even more "what it is": a being which aspires to something beyond what has been existentially given. It does not merely grow "toward" Being. It also communicates to us in an unusually eloquent way its aspiration to complete itself within us.

What distinguishes us from the insects about which Caillois writes is also neither a greater authenticity nor an epistemological superiority. It is, rather, a deficit in another kind of knowledge, one which is not so much cognitive as "existential." At the level of our own bodily morphology and markings we, too, intend toward appearance; we, too, solicit the visual affirmation which we need to be "ourselves." However, whereas the insect might be said to "know" what it wants, we do not. This is because the flexibility and agency we have gained within the domains of the social and the erotic by playing with the masks we assume have been achieved at the cost of what might be called a radical "ontological *méconnaissance*." Our capacity to manipulate the images through which we are seen has led us to believe that we are purely and simply what Lacan tells us we are: beings who lack "being."[19] We have lost sight of the fact that we are also beings who lack Being.

Finally, it is not through the intervention of the gaze that this last lack can be satisfied. Even if the gaze were to ratify us in the guise of that image through which we most deeply yearn to be apprehended, we would not appear and so Be. It is only the human look which can confer upon us that more-than-reality to which we too, without knowing it, formally aspire, and it is only by speaking its very own language of desire that it can do so. This does not mean, however, that we are the blank surface onto which the desiring look can project whatever it wants. Regardless of whether it transpires at the site of a human or a nonhuman form, appearance always begins with the self-manifestation of the perceptual object.

RECIPIENTS OF APPEARANCE

In arguing that objects not only direct themselves toward perceiving subjects, but that they also initiate that complex event which I am calling "appearance," I am again drawing in part upon Arendt and Portmann. At the beginning of the first chapter of *The Life of the Mind*, Arendt refers twice to the perceiving subject as a "recipient of appearance" (19). Conceptualizing this transaction from the other end, Portmann characterizes self-showing as a "conveyance for receivers."[20] Here, however, I have also been anticipated by a number of other thinkers. Heidegger, Lacan, and Merleau-Ponty also insist upon the chronological priority of self-display over seeing.

Heidegger, who maintains that "self-showing appearance is the mark of the presence and absence of everything that is present, of every kind and rank," adds that "even when Showing is accomplished by our human saying, even then this showing, this pointer, is preceded by an indication that it will let itself be shown."[21] Similarly, in his study of the field of vision, Lacan suggests that when we look we are not leading, but rather following what we see. Although this truth is elided in our waking lives, it makes itself available every time we dream.[22]

Merleau-Ponty, for whom the visual is also the primary domain for the disclosure of Being, maintains that we might be said to find our own look in the things at which we look—that the seer, in effect, uncoils herself from the spectacle. "[I]t is the painter to whom the things of the world give birth by a sort of concentration or coming-to-itself of the visible," he writes in "Eye and Mind."[23] He makes the same claim in *Phenomenology of Perception*, and in terms which are even more germane to the present discussion: "every perception is a communication or a communion, the taking up or completion by us of some extraneous intention."[24]

It might seem as if things and nonhuman creatures are without the semiotic means to communicate to us more than a vague appeal to look at them. Consequently, even if they "direct" our look, as Portmann puts it, they must do so blindly. They cannot specify how we are to engage with them visually. However, running like a leitmotif through the work of almost all the writers who have figured in this discussion so far is an insistence upon the capacity of creatures and things to tell us how we should look at them.

In *Parmenides*, Heidegger writes that the look that we "perform" in relation to others is always a response to their look at us.[25] They might be said to provide us with the inspiration, capacity, and wherewithal for looking at them in the way in which they intend. The look, Heidegger tells us in the same text, was a signifier for the Greeks for the "countenance" or "outward look" of a self-showing creature or thing (104). We, too, should understand the countenance or outward appearance of others as the means whereby they communicate with us. It is out of the "ordinary" surface of things that the divine or "uncanny" shines forth: that the Being we are to confer upon others reveals itself to us (ibid.).

Heidegger reserves for other human beings the capacity to disclose their essence in this way to us (ibid.). He also accounts for self-showing in strangely monolithic terms: it is seemingly always with the same initiating gift that appearance begins. There is consequently no possibility within this philosophical model for conceptualizing the Being which we bestow upon creatures and things as something which emerges from them in their phenomenological particularity.[26] Arendt, Portmann, and Merleau-Ponty, however, attribute to animals as well as humans the capacity to communicate to the human look how they intend to be seen, and suggest that it is precisely through their formal properties that they do so.

Arendt maintains that the essence of things lies at the surface; it is for her there, and there alone, that the truth of a being is to be found (26–32). To affirm beings in their Being can consequently only mean to celebrate them in all of their superficial beauty. Similarly, as we have seen, Portmann proposes that what animals solicit from the look is an acknowledgment of their "form value" (214). When we look at creatures and things in the way that permits them to appear, our look comes to rest precisely at the level of their aesthetic properties—color, morphology, markings. For Merleau-Ponty, to look is to find the solution to a "sensible datum."[27] It is also in finding this solution that the seer finds her own vision. As Merleau-Ponty puts it in *Phenomenology of Perception*, "to learn to see colors . . . is to acquire a certain style of seeing" (153).

THE COMMUNICATION OF FORM

At one moment in *The Writing of Stones*, Caillois refers to rock patterns as an "extraordinary [congress] of signs" (95).[28] He thereby suggests that we learn to look at creatures and things in the way they aim to be seen by "reading" them. However, Caillois does not merely attribute to stone patterns the status of a language. He also says that they constitute an extraordinary congress of signs *"which have no meaning"* (ibid.; his emphasis). This claim is at first glance nonsensical. We are not always in possession of the key by means of which to access a sign's meaning. Therefore, certain signs do not speak to us. Nevertheless, when face to face with a sign, we are always sure that meaning is somehow "there," even if hidden or buried. This is because our everyday way of thinking about a sign is precisely as something within which meaning "resides." What does it mean to refer to a form or a pattern as a sign when it is devoid even of this semantic latency? And how can we "read" signs which do not mean?

Portmann and Merleau-Ponty provide a structuralist answer to the last question. Portmann suggests that, although lacking a signifier/signified division, animal patterns constitute a language because there, as in human language, we find a play of differences. Like words, animal patterns derive their value through their reference to a paradigmatic field (46–47); they emerge against the backdrops of genus, species, and even the larger animal kingdom. This language is not, however, immediately discernible. In order to understand it, we need the assistance of zoology. "Insight into the sequence of developmental stages and into structural principles enriches the appearance of an animal form for the person looking at it," writes Portmann, "since signs from its outward aspect will speak to him as silent, unobtrusive witnesses of a hidden order in organic form" (46–47).

Whereas Portmann stresses difference and systematicity when trying to make sense of the signlike nature of objects, Merleau-Ponty stresses similarity and uniqueness. For him, a given body becomes recognizable as a sign not at the moment that it is situated within the larger system of its species, but rather at the moment that one grasps it as a series of correspondences. These correspondences are, moreover, unique to that object alone; they consequently constitute more a personal language than elements of a *langue*. Merleau-Ponty suggests that every body speaks by means of the unique equivalences which obtain between one of its attributes and all of the others. Each part of any given body is so symptomatic of the whole that it could be said to provide a variant of every other part. The gesture which one part makes finds its correlative in the sound with which another part reverberates, and the color with which a third shines. "A woman passing by is not first and foremost a corporeal contour for me, a colored mannequin, or a spectacle, . . ." Merleau-Ponty writes in "Indirect Language and the Voices of Silence." "She is a certain manner of being flesh which is given entirely in her walk or even in the simple click of her heel on the ground, just as the tension of the bow is present in each fiber of wood—a most remarkable variant of the norm of walking, looking, touching, and speaking."[29]

Sometimes, Merleau-Ponty maintains that this language "teaches itself" to the one who observes it.[30] At other times, though, he suggests that it is recognizable only to those who speak an equivalent language. Although, in Merleau-Ponty's account, each body's system of correspondences is unique to it alone, there are always perceptual subjects within which that system finds answering reverberations. For each of us, there are certain textures, certain forms, and certain nuances that we find, quite simply, "moving." "[Certain things] have an internal equivalent in me," Merleau-Ponty writes in "Eye and Mind"; "they arouse in me a carnal formula of their presence" (126). He makes the same point via two other metaphors in an earlier text. One perceives "effectively" only if the perceived phenomenon "finds an echo within [one]," he writes there— only if there is a "synchroniz[ation]" of seer and seen.[31]

As the words "echo" and "synchronization" suggest, the kind of communication that Merleau-Ponty imagines taking place between perceptual subject and perceptual object is formal rather than ideational. The psyche has no role to play in the establishment of the equivalences through which the seen "speaks" to the seer. This translation is a strictly bodily affair. This is not an oversight on Merleau-Ponty's part, but a deliberate exclusion. The author of *Phenomenology of Perception* dreams not only of a smooth conversion from spectacle to spectator, but also of their absolute correlation. This correlation can only be guaranteed so long as what is seen is not "a meaning for the understanding," but rather "a structure accessible to inspection by the body" (320). Only so long as the psyche is absent can the perceptual object and the perceiving subject be transparently accessible to each other.

Leo Bersani, another major theorist of the phenomenal world, shares Merleau-Ponty's interest in bodily equivalences. In a number of books either written by him alone, or coauthored with Ulysse Dutoit, Bersani—who has been for over ten years my most important intellectual interlocutor—has theorized what he calls the "communication of forms."[32] As its name suggests, the communication of forms is not semantic, but rather corporeal.[33] It occurs either when the form of one thing speaks to the form of another, or when the elements of a single form speak among themselves.[34] In *The Culture of Redemption*, Bersani suggests that it is through human memory that these affinities are established (74). Later, however, he denies that the psyche has any role to play in the communication of forms. In *Homos*, Bersani maintains that it is primarily via sexuality that this exchange occurs (120–25). In *Caravaggio's Secrets*, he and Dutoit associate it in some more general way with the movement in space of one body toward another (35, 72).

Whereas Merleau-Ponty's foreclosure of the psyche might be said to have been motivated by a desire for presence, Bersani's is ethical. For the author of *The Culture of Redemption* and *Arts of Impoverishment*, there can be no tenable psychic relation between subject and world; it is only hatred that leads one subject to take cognizance of another. This is because identity reigns supreme at the level of the psyche, and identity can sustain itself only through the murderous incorporation of the other.[35] Corporeal convergence is able to effect what the convergence of body and psyche cannot because, as Bersani puts it in *Homos*, the subject is at such moments "so obscenely 'rubbed' by the object it anticipates mastering that the very boundaries separating subject from object, boundaries necessary for possession, [are] erased" (100).[36]

The dissolution of identity about which Bersani writes in *Homos* is no more lasting than the erotic encounter through which it is effected. However, when one body moves away from another, it leaves behind what might be called the "traces of difference." When the now solitary subject attempts to reconstitute itself, these traces of difference stick in the gears of the egoic machinery. The result is an inaccurate self-replication. In *Arts of Impoverishment*, Bersani and Dutoit dream of setting in motion an infinite series of these inaccurate self-replications (6–7). In *Homos*, Bersani intimates that inaccurate self-replication might also lead to an appetite for alterity, and so to a different relation to other creatures and things (146).

Both in *Caravaggio's Secrets* and a conversation for *October* with Tim Dean, Hal Foster, and me, Bersani suggests that at the moment that one body meets another in space, the illusion of lack is also dispelled. We then understand that we are not—as we have imagined—isolated from other creatures and things, but in a state of perpetual implicit communication with other forms.[37] In *Caravaggio's Secrets*, Bersani and Dutoit write that "there are no gaps, no empty spaces, in creation. We are not *cut off* from anything; nothing escapes connectedness, the play of and between forms" (72).

In the final pages of this book, I will be elaborating a very different account of how we read signs which have no meaning than that variously provided by Portmann, Merleau-Ponty, and Bersani. What follows, however, will communicate in profound ways with what might be called the "form" of Bersani's argument.

LETTING THE LANDSCAPE SPEAK ITSELF
IN US

It is not by responding to the formal parameters of another being at the level of our own objectivity that we communicate with it; were we ever to succeed in synchronizing ourselves in this way with another creature or thing, the result would be a monologue, not a dialogue. We communicate with the world only when we enable its forms to signify—only when we provide the meaning they lack. I say "lack" because phenomenal forms are not simply meaningless signs; they are also signs in search of significance. But it is in fact through an abundance rather than a deficit that phenomenal forms address us. They are "pregnant" with a beauty to which only a very special kind of human signification can give birth. And only by becoming "ourselves" can we provide that signification.

In "Cézanne's Doubt," Merleau-Ponty attributes to Cézanne an extraordinary claim: "The landscape thinks itself in me, and I am its consciousness" (67). With this real or mythical pronouncement,[38] Cézanne imputes to the world an aspiration toward something which it does not itself possess, something which we alone can provide. Cézanne calls this faculty "consciousness." However, what "consciousness" really means in this context is not intellection, but rather the transfigurative act of vision through which the prospect which unfolded itself before the painter became the prospect on his canvas. And what enabled this act of vision was not consciousness, but rather paint and libido.

With the sentence assigned to him by Merleau-Ponty, Cézanne might also be said to abdicate or "lay down" the gaze.[39] Rather than aspiring to become the initiator of perception, he gladly accepts his role as recipient. This is because he understands better than most spectators what it means to look. "It is not with me that my paintings originate," Cézanne in effect claims; "In a certain sense, I am not even the painter of my paintings. I am, rather, the medium through which the things of the world paint themselves."

The words Merleau-Ponty attributes to Cézanne contain in a

condensed and allegorical form my entire theory of appearance. When we look, in the most profound and creative sense of that word, we are always responding to a prior solicitation from other creatures and things. This solicitation is aesthetic in nature: the world addresses us through its formal parameters. However, in displaying their colors, shapes, patterns and movements to us, things do not merely request us to turn our eyes toward them, or even to answer in kind. What the world of phenomenal forms solicits from us is our desire.

This might seem a contradiction in terms. Human, animal, insect, and stone colors, patterns, and shapes constitute a self-showing. There is thus no *différance*—no delay separating sign from referent—in the case of phenomenal signification. The language of things is a language of presence. Desire, on the other hand, is virtually synonymous with absence. It is only through the "fading" of our "being"[40] that each of us is inducted into this fundamentally visual language. It is also by making a perceptual stimulus the signifier of our past—by temporalizing it—that we engage in a libidinal speech act. However, what I am calling "appearance" occurs only through that most paradoxical of all events: the meeting of absence and presence.

Creatures and things do not solicit desire in the abstract. Rather, what they seek from us is that very particular passion of the signifier through which we have individuated what is common to all subjects: the loss of *das Ding*. The phenomenal forms of the world invite us to make them part of our singular language of desire—to make them components of the rhetoric through which we "care." What enables us to do so are the similarities and contiguities linking the shapes, patterns, colors and movements of the creatures and things we have loved in the past to those of the creatures and things which manifest themselves to us in the present.

It is out of an ontological rather than a semiotic imperative that the world solicits us to desire it in this way. This is because it is only by being lifted out of the real and into the more-than-reality of a singular constellation of perceptual memories that the world can Be. However, we do not confer Being upon creatures and things simply by finding affinities between them and what we have previously perceived, any more than we do when we look at them in an everyday way, or find bodily correspondences between themselves and ourselves. We look in the way that makes appearance possible only when we also allow the perceptual present to *reincarnate* or *recorporealize* the past—to give it a *new form*. We only give the gift of Being to something when we permit it *inaccurately* to replicate what was.

Absence and presence can only meet in this transformative way when the perceiving subject is "open" to the perceptual object. To be "open" in this way means to renounce all claim to be the master of one's own language of desire. It means, indeed, to surrender one's signifying repository to the world, to become the space within which the world itself speaks. To abdicate enunciatory control in this way is, however, not to lose, but rather to find one's language of desire. This is because we cannot consciously choose the visual "words" through which our past will be respoken, or what creatures and things we will bring into the metaphoric light. All that we can do is answer the appeal which comes to us from the world to find our memories in its forms.

But although it is less we ourselves than the world that finally speaks our language of desire, we cannot provide the opening within which other creatures and things appear without giving them a meaning which is specific to ourselves, one which they cannot anticipate. We cannot confer Being upon the world without appropriating it, carrying it away from itself, conferring upon it a supplemental value. The world "knows" this. It does not circumscribe in any way the meaning which we can give to it. All it asks us to do is to look at it first.

SINGING THE SONG OF BEAUTY

The world intends to be seen not just by one, but rather by an infinity of eyes. This is in part because no creature or thing can find an answering set of equivalences in every subject. As all of us know, some objects speak our language and others do not. The pleasure we take in looking at certain beings is infinite. The style of others fails to move us. From yet others, we cannot help but avert our eyes. Fortunately, vision is finally as manifold as are beings themselves.

The world also intends to be seen by an infinity of eyes because even those creatures and things at which we look with pleasure exceed our capacity to see them. As Merleau-Ponty puts it, everything that reveals itself to the look has a "behind" and "after."[41] This is in part because we do not stand in front of the world, as if before a picture; rather, we are *inside* it, and our interior vantage point serves not only to disclose certain aspects of what we look at, but also to conceal others. It is, in addition, because beings do not always display themselves in the same way to the look; they are constantly moving, and with each move what they show changes. Some new aspect comes into view and a previous one slips into invisibility. Perspective is consequently a feature not only of the look, but of objects as well.[42]

I like to think that the inexhaustible richness of creatures and things also derives from the relationship between their language and ours. If the significance which we find within them were already latent within them, we would be able to exhaust it with our perceptual and linguistic signifiers. However, they are pregnant not with meaning, but with *beauty*. Our capacity to signify beauty has no limits. It is born of a loss which can never be adequately named, and whose consequence is, quite simply, the human imperative to engage in a ceaseless signification. It is finally this never-ending symbolization that the world wants from us. It is a call to which none of us is adequate by ourselves; we are finite beings, beings who cannot help but come to an end. Only as a collectivity can we be equal to the demand not only to find beauty in all of the world's forms, but to sing forever and in a constantly new way the jubilant song of that beauty.

NOTES

CHAPTER I: *Seeing for the Sake of Seeing*

1. See, for instance, Friedrich Nietzsche, *The Will to Power*, trans. Walter Kaufmann and R. J. Hollingdale (New York: Vintage, 1967), pp. 305–31; and Hannah Arendt, *The Life of the Mind* (New York: Harcourt, Brace, 1978), pp. 19–40.

2. I say "Plato's Socrates" rather than "Plato" so as to hold open two possibilities: the possibility on the one hand that the central character in Plato's Socratic dialogues does not always speak for Plato himself, and the possibility on the other that he does not always articulate the views of the historical Socrates. I want to voice my reluctance, however, to insist too hard upon the distinction between Plato's Socrates and Plato himself, since—whether or not it is based upon a questionable authorial imputation—what the first of these figures says has been so determinative for what we think of as "Platonism." This Platonism, moreover, represents more than a set of philosophical assumptions; it has been (and continues to be) a real force in the world. Some classicists are prepared, however, to draw a much more emphatic line between Plato's Socrates and Plato himself. Drew A. Hyland, for instance, argues in *Finitude and Transcendence in the Platonic Dialogues* (Albany: State University of New York Press, 1995) that in each Platonic dialogue the conversation takes place between "certain character types." Moreover, "each person and each situation is so presented that the thoughtful reader can notice what can be revealed by (and to) that person with that standpoint, and also what is, what perhaps must be, concealed" (154). James A. Arieti maintains that the Platonic dialogues are not philosophical texts at all, but dramas with characters and actions (see *Interpreting Plato: The Dialogues as Drama* [Savage, Md.:

Rowman and Littlefield, 1991]). I will henceforth refer to Plato's Socrates simply as "Socrates."

3. See the *Republic*, book 7. The translation used in this chapter for all citations from the *Republic* will be that rendered by G. M. A. Grube and revised by C. D. C. Reeve. This translation can be found in Plato, *Complete Works*, ed. John M. Cooper and D. S. Hutchinson (Indianapolis: Hackett, 1997).

4. I quote here from Socrates' account of opinion in book 6 of the *Republic*. Opinion is the intellectual faculty which the prisoners exercise when they attribute reality to the cave shadows (516d).

5. This is how Socrates characterizes the Good in the *Republic*, book 6, 508a–d, and book 7, 516a–b and 532a–c.

6. See Friedrich Nietzsche, *The Gay Science*, trans. Walter Kaufmann (New York: Vintage, 1974), esp. pp. 181–82.

7. Martin Heidegger, "Plato's Doctrine of Truth," trans. Thomas Sheehan, in Heidegger, *Pathmarks*, ed. William McNeill (Cambridge: Cambridge University Press, 1998), pp. 155–82. In Heidegger's view, the parable of the cave dramatizes the philosophical shift away from the first of these notions to the second. Heidegger makes clear his commitment to the conceptualization of truth as the unhiding of the hidden.

8. For Arendt's deconstruction of the two-world theory, see *The Life of the Mind*, pp. 3–65.

9. I take the phrase "world spectator"—but not the meaning that I give to it—from Arendt. She uses it in her *Lectures on Kant's Political Philosophy*, ed. Ronald Beiner (Chicago: University of Chicago Press, 1982), p. 44, in the context of discussing Kantian cosmopolitanism. She indicates her strong preference there for the notion of the world spectator over that of the world citizen. For Arendt, the latter makes no sense, because a citizen is someone with territorially limited "responsibilities, obligations, and rights." A world spectator is apparently someone who "goes visiting" (43), but retains these responsibilities, obligations, and rights.

10. Hannah Arendt, "Philosophy and Politics," *Social Research* 57, no. 1 (1990): 94.

11. Arendt, *The Life of the Mind*, pp. 19–23.

12. Martin Heidegger, "Letter on Humanism," in *Basic Writings*, ed. Davis Farrell Krell (San Francisco: HarperSanFrancisco, 1993), pp. 217–65.

13. See, for instance, Martin Heidegger, *On the Way to Language*, trans. Peter D. Hertz (San Francisco: HarperSanFrancisco, 1971); "Building Dwelling Thinking," in Martin Heidegger, *Poetry, Language, Thought*,

trans. Albert Hofstadter (New York: Harper and Row, 1971), pp. 143–61; and ". . . Poetically Man Dwells . . . ," in Heidegger, *Poetry, Language, Thought*, pp. 211–29.

14. See, for instance, Hannah Arendt, *The Human Condition* (Chicago: University of Chicago Press, 1958), pp. 192, 198–99, and 204; and *On Revolution* (New York: Viking, 1963), pp. 99–109. Only in the opening section of *The Life of the Mind* does Arendt theorize appearance in unambiguously visual terms.

15. Martin Heidegger, *An Introduction to Metaphysics*, trans. Ralph Manheim (New Haven, Conn.: Yale University Press, 1959), p. 66.

16. Interestingly, Timaeus suggests in the *Timaeus* that space is strictly an earthly affair. It is the "location for all things that come to be," and it is apprehended by "a kind of bastard reasoning" (see *Timaeus*, trans. Donald J. Zeyl, in Plato, *Complete Works*, ed. Cooper and Hutchinson, 52a–b). One's spatial coordinates would thus seem one of the first things to be lost when effecting a philosophical ascent. Curiously, though, Timaeus does not effect the close join of these coordinates with the look which one would expect, and upon which I am insisting. He says the apprehension of space does "not involve sense perception" (52a, b). I will be using Zeyl's translation for all future quotations from the *Timaeus*.

17. Jill Stouffer, one of my classical Greek advisors, tells me that a literal transcription of the original text here would be "relinquish their eyes and other senses." But the fact that vision is individually named, whereas the other senses are collectively invoked, clearly indicates that the primary sacrifice is visual.

18. Thus arriving at what Socrates calls "belief" is a precondition for the subsequent movement to "thought," and the movement to "thought" a precondition for the subsequent movement to "understanding." The logic here would seem similar to that operative within Diotima's account of the ladder leading from physical to spiritual beauty. I draw here upon Julia Annas's very detailed and helpful discussion of the differences between the metaphors of the cave and the line in "Understanding the Good: Sun, Line, and Cave," in *Plato's Republic: Critical Essays*, ed. Richard Kraut (Boulder, Colo.: Rowman and Littlefield, 1997), pp. 143–68.

19. As Drew A. Hyland argues in *Finitude and Transcendence in the Platonic Dialogues*: "For something to be brought to unhiddenness someone must be looking" (144).

20. *Symposium* 210a–212b. Unless specified otherwise, the translation of this dialogue which will be used here is that provided by Alexander

Nehamas and Paul Woodruff in Plato, *Complete Works*, ed. Cooper and Hutchinson.

21. In 201.d Socrates repeats what Diotima—a "woman of Mantinea," who "was wise about many things besides this"—has told him. Since what Socrates says is itself repeated by Apollodorus in the *Symposium*, the case could be made that Plato takes particular care to differentiate himself from the words Socrates utters here. Nevertheless, at least one classical scholar has recently advanced a contrary argument. Alexander Nehamas suggests that the fact that Socrates derives this story from Diotima connects it more to Plato than to Socrates. As he points out in *Virtues of Authenticity: Essays on Plato and Socrates* (Princeton, N.J.: Princeton University Press, 1999), p. 304, Socrates' claim that he cannot understand Diotima (206b) and Diotima's warning that Socrates "may not be capable of being initiated into 'the final and highest mystery' of love (210a) may well both be Plato's way of indicating that the views involved toward the end of Socrates' speech are not Socrates' but Plato's own."

22. In his commentary on Plato's *Symposium*, in *The Dialogues of Plato*, vol. 2, trans. R. E. Allen (New Haven, Conn.: Yale University Press, 1991), Allen writes that "Beauty is treated as equivalent to Goodness" in this dialogue. Moreover, "the ascent passage in the *Symposium* looks forward to the *Republic* and the comparison of the Good to the Sun" (85).

23. I draw in this paragraph on Michael Joyce's translation of the *Symposium*; see Plato, *The Collected Dialogues*, ed. Edith Hamilton and Huntington Cairns (Princeton, N.J.: Princeton University Press, 1989), p. 562. Alexander Nehamas and Paul Woodruff render the passage from which I have just excerpted in the following way:

> [The Form of Beauty] *is* and neither comes to be nor passes away, neither waxes or wanes . . . it is not beautiful this way and ugly that way, nor beautiful at one time and ugly at another, nor beautiful in relation to one thing and ugly in relation to another; nor is it beautiful here but ugly there, as it would be if it were beautiful for some people and ugly for others. Nor will the beautiful appear to him in the guise of a face or hands or anything else that belongs to the body. It will not appear to him as one idea or one kind of knowledge. It is not anywhere in another thing . . . but itself by itself with itself, it is always one in form. (211a, b)

From *Phaedrus*, trans. Alexander Nehamas and Paul Woodruff, in Cooper and Hutchinson. Here and elsewhere I will be using Nehamas and Woodruff's translation of this dialogue.

24. Shadi Bartsch has recently argued that the equation between eros and the look is an insistent one in classical literature, both in the Greek and the Roman traditions. See "The Philosopher as Narcissist: Knowing Onself in Classical Antiquity," in Robert S. Nelson, ed., *Seeing As Others Saw: Visuality Before and Beyond the Renaissance* (Cambridge: Cambridge University Press, forthcoming). The equation is not always elaborated in such negative terms.

25. R. E. Allen also remarks upon this metaphysical trajectory of the *Symposium* (77–78). However, it seems to pose no problem for him, since in his view—as in Diotima's—the "proper object of love" is that which *is*, rather than that which merely *seems* (104). This valorization of Socratic Being vitiates what is in a number of other respects a very fine reading of the *Symposium*. For William S. Cobb, in "Commentary on the *Symposium*," in *Plato's Erotic Dialogues*, trans. William S. Cobb (Albany: State University of New York, 1993), there apparently is no metaphysical trajectory in the *Symposium* for us either to applaud or to worry about. Diotima's "ideal lover is very much engaged in the world, practicing the virtues of ordinary life, ordering cities and households and engaging in useful conversations" (76).

26. For Martha C. Nussbaum, the *Phaedrus* offers a much less qualified appreciation of human beauty than the one I find there. She maintains in *The Fragility of Goodness: Luck and Ethics in Greek Tragedy and Philosophy* (Cambridge: Cambridge University Press, 1986), that, "instead of loving one another as exemplars of beauty and goodness, properties which they might conceivably lose without ceasing to be themselves," the lovers described by Socrates in his second speech "love one another's character, memories, and aspirations—which are, as Aristotle too will say, what each person is 'in and of himself'" (220). In their introduction to the *Phaedrus*, Nehamas and Woodruff advance a claim which is more in the spirit of the present discussion: "Eros . . . is losing one's mind to Beauty. It is superficially directed at the boy, but the ultimate driving force behind it is the recollection of and the desire to possess again the Beauty which the soul saw during its disembodied travels. Moreover, Beauty itself is a proxy for the rest of the Forms, which it helps us to recollect, however imperfectly, and which it makes us desire all the more" (xxiii).

27. *Phaedrus* 250b–c.

28. For two powerful indictments of Plato's instrumentalization of eros, and ones with which I am in profound sympathy, see Gregory Vlastos, in "The Individual As Object of Love in Plato," *Platonic Studies* (Princeton,

N.J.: Princeton University Press, 1981), pp. 3–34; and Page DuBois, *Sappho Is Burning* (Chicago: Chicago University Press, 1995), pp. 77–97.

29. In the passage upon which I draw here, the lover functions as a mirror in which the loved one sees himself. However, this "self" is itself a delayed reflection of heavenly beauty. Consequently, in loving the lover, the loved one also "has no idea what he loves" (255d).

30. As will become evident later in this chapter, "ownness" signifies for me not the triumph of the ego, but rather its obverse.

31. See Walter Benjamin, "On Some Motifs in Baudelaire," in *Illuminations*, ed. Hannah Arendt, trans. Harry Zorn (London: Fontana, 1973), p. 183.

32. When Socrates relates the parable of the cave, he only refers to the prisoner's return to the cave as a speculative possibility (516e). However, when he interprets this part of the allegory, the return to the cave becomes an imperative. "It is our task as founders . . . to compel the best natures to reach the study we said before is the most important," he tells Glaucon, "namely, to make the ascent and see the good. But when they've made it and looked sufficiently, we mustn't allow them to do what they're allowed to do today. . . . To stay there and refuse to go down again to the prisoners in the cave . . ." (519c–d). This is because the primary concern of the *Republic* is with the *socius*, not the individual.

33. Sigmund Freud, *The Ego and the Id, in The Standard Edition of the Complete Psychological Works*, trans. James Strachey (London: Hogarth, 1961), vol. 19, pp. 40–59.

34. Socrates solicits Timaeus's speech, never interrupts it, and allows Timaeus to have the last word in the dialogue.

35. Socrates privileges oneness at every point of his discourse in the *Republic*, from his account of Goodness, to his account of the ideal republic, to his account of what a man should be. Since only the first of these topics is germane to the present discussion, I will content myself with pointing out that the trajectory traced by the parable of the cave is a movement from a multiplicity of shadows, about which there also seems to be a diversity of opinion, to the brilliance of a single solar body, the sun, which is itself capable of determining how it is to be seen.

36. Luce Irigaray, *Speculum of the Other Woman*, trans. Gillian G. Gill (Ithaca, N.Y.: Cornell University Press, 1985), p. 266.

37. The metaphor is Gillian G. Gill's. It does not appear in the French text.

38. It might seem surprising that I would draw here on Lacan's seventh seminar, which has been published in English under the title *The*

Seminar of Jacques Lacan, Book VII: The Ethics of Psychoanalysis, 1959–1960, trans. Dennis Porter (New York: Norton, 1992), rather than his untranslated eighth, in which he provides an extended reading of Plato's *Symposium*. However, much as I admire the eighth seminar, I find its account of desire finally less compelling than that offered in the seventh for two important reasons. First, in *Le Séminaire, livre VIII: Le transfert*, ed. Jacques-Alain Miller (Paris: Editions du Seuil, 1991), pp. 163–95, Lacan suggests that the hidden prototype behind Socrates' Good is not *das Ding*, impossible nonobject of desire, but rather the *objet a*. He also insists upon the phallus as the *objet a* par excellence. In so doing, Lacan undoes the extraordinarily liberating account of desire which he had offered the previous year.

39. Although it is Lacan himself who teaches us this, he is not always as careful as he might be in maintaining the absolute unspecifiability of *das Ding*. Sometimes, he—like Irigaray—attributes to it a maternal identity. See, for instance, *The Seminar of Jacques Lacan, Book VII*, p. 68.

40. Although the issue of *das Ding* is one to which Lacan frequently returns in *The Seminar of Jacques Lacan, Book VII*, his most extensive treatment of it occurs on pp. 43–84, 101–114, and 129–30. For his association of displacement away from *das Ding* with illumination, see p. 58–59.

41. Sigmund Freud, *Beyond the Pleasure Principle*, in *The Standard Edition*, vol. 18, p. 42.

42. Jacques Lacan, "Function and Field of Speech and Language in Psychoanalysis," in *Écrits: A Selection*, trans. Alan Sheridan (New York: Norton, 1977), p. 65. Lacan also often refers to what is lost through symbolization as "being." Wherever I use this latter word in a Lacanian sense, I will enclose it in quotation marks.

43. *The Seminar of Jacques Lacan, Book VII*, pp. 19–127. For an elaboration of the notion of a libidinal speech act, see Chapters 2, 3, and 5 of this volume.

44. Lacan also equates the *jouissance* which accompanies the undoing of the signifier with a "will to destruction." See *The Seminar of Jacques Lacan, Book VII*, p. 212.

45. I am invoking here Stanley Fish's book *Self-Consuming Artifact: The Experience of Seventeenth-Century Literature* (Berkeley: University of California Press, 1972).

46. As we learn in Lacan's "Function and Field of Speech and Language in Psychoanalysis," in *Écrits*, pp. 30–113, this is one of the main reasons why Lacanian psychoanalysis directs itself against the imaginary.

47. In addition to the passage quoted above, see pp. 115–27, 213–14, and 227.

48. Genesis 1.3. I am relying here upon the translation of Genesis provided by *The New Oxford Annotated Bible*, ed. Bruce M. Metzger and Roland E. Murphy (New York: Harcourt Brace Jovanovich, 1991).

49. For a careful elaboration of the limitations to which our speech acts are subject, see Judith Butler, *Excitable Speech* (New York: Routledge, 1997).

50. As I will attempt to demonstrate in Chapter 6, such an occurrence is by no means dependent upon divine intervention. The world itself participates in its display. Indeed, it is always a co-actant in the event I am calling "appearance."

51. Socrates does not explicitly say that the prisoner informs his companions about the region above, but he implies that the latter does so, since he describes the other prisoners as understanding that he has made an "upward journey" (517a).

52. Socrates characterizes the verbal exchanges between the prisoners as a possibility rather than a certainty. He writes: "And if they could talk to one another . . . " (515b). However, much of the allegory he relates is dependent upon the assumption that the prisoners do in fact speak.

53. See, for instance, Martin Heidegger, *Being and Time*, trans. John Macquarrie and Edward Robinson (San Francisco: HarperSanFrancisco, 1962), p. 78; and Martin Heidegger, *History of the Concept of Time*, trans. Theodore Kisiel (Bloomington: Indiana University Press, 1992), pp. 156–60.

54. For a clarification of the meaning of *Dasein*, see Chapter 2.

55. "Care" is a Heideggerian concept, which figures centrally in *Being and Time*. I will be inflecting it here in some quite un-Heideggerian ways.

56. The concept of presence-at-hand derives from Heidegger. For a basic definition of it, see *Being and Time*, p. 42.

57. As Heidegger observes in *The Concept of Time*, "No one is himself in everydayness. What someone is, and how he is, is nobody: no one and yet everyone with one another. . . . This nobody by whom we ourselves are lived in *everydayness* is the ['they']." *The Concept of Time*, trans. William McNeill (Oxford: Blackwell, 1992), pp. 8e–9e.

58. Hannah Arendt, *Love and Saint Augustine*, ed. Joanna Vecchiarelli Scott and Judith Chelius Stark (Chicago: University of Chicago Press, 1996), p. 18.

59. This might seem a very Socratic formulation. Socrates tells us in the *Phaedrus*, after all, that the one who loves what is perfect also becomes perfect (250c). However, in Socrates' account, the lover comes to resemble what he loves through the renunciation of all personal agency—by achiev-

ing in relation to the Form of the Good or of Beauty a complete receptivity. In my account, love represents not a passive assimilation of the love-object, but rather the active illumination of the love-object through a visual symbolization. It is through the kinds of symbolizations which we effect that we individuate ourselves both from each other, and from the "they."

60. Heidegger, *The Concept of Time*, pp. 13e–14e.

61. Heidegger, *Being and Time*, p. 41.

62. Arendt also insists upon the importance for the world of there being a plurality of looks. In *The Human Condition*, she writes: "Only where things can be seen by many in a variety of aspects without changing their identity, so that those who are gathered around them know they see sameness in utter diversity, can worldly reality truly and reliably appear" (p. 57).

63. Many of us find the idea of an unqualified affirmation of the world monstrous. After all, not every action is worthy of applause, nor every creature of our appreciation. But as Nietzsche himself makes clear, the danger which confronts us is not that we will find too many things beautiful, but rather too few.

64. This is a point emphasized by Heidegger in *Parmenides*, trans. André Schuwer and Richard Rojcewicz (Bloomington: Indiana University Press, 1992), pp. 13 and 62–63.

65. William J. Richardson, "Psychoanalysis and the Being-question," in *Interpreting Lacan*, ed. Joseph H. Smith and William Kerrigan (New Haven, Conn.: Yale University Press, 1983), pp. 139–59.

66. Martin Heidegger, "The Age of the World Picture," in *The Question Concerning Technology and Other Essays*, trans. William Lovitt (New York: Harper and Row, 1977), pp. 115–54; and "The Question Concerning Technology," in *The Question Concerning Technology and Other Essays*, pp. 3–35.

67. Martin Heidegger, "What Is Metaphysics?" in *Basic Writings*, p. 110.

68. I draw in part here upon Lacan's second seminar. See especially *The Seminar of Jacques Lacan, Book II: The Ego in Freud's Theory and in the Technique of Psychoanalysis, 1954–55*, trans. Sylvana Tomaselli (New York: Norton, 1991), pp. 165–71. It is, however, within the seventh rather than the second seminar that Lacan theorizes not only the void which resides at the center of subjectivity, but also the crucial part played within the operations of desire by the impossible nonobject or no-thing of desire.

CHAPTER 2: *Eating the Book*

1. Sigmund Freud, *Psycho-Analytic Notes on an Autobiographical Account of a Case of Paranoia*, in *The Standard Edition of the Complete Psychological Works*, trans. James Strachey (London: Hogarth, 1958), vol. 12, pp. 69–70.

2. This passage comes from Goethe's *Faust*, part 1, scene 4. It has been translated from German into English by Bayard Taylor and modified by James Strachey.

3. For this definition of "subject," see Martin Heidegger, "The Age of the World Picture," in *The Question Concerning Technology and Other Essays*, trans. William Lovitt (New York: Harper and Row, 1977), 115–54; "The Word of Nietzsche," in *The Question Concerning Technology and Other Essays*, pp. 87–90; and *Nietzsche*, trans. Joan Stambaugh, David Farrell Krell, and Frank A. Capuzzi (San Francisco: HarperSanFrancisco, 1987), vols. 3 and 4. Already in *Being and Time* (trans. John Macquarrie and Edward Robinson [San Francisco: HarperSanFrancisco, 1962]), p. 150, Heidegger indicates that for him "subject" implies a substantializing notion of personhood, and one entirely alien to the ontology of *Dasein*.

4. I am seemingly imputing to Heidegger an intention which is at odds with what he himself much later said on the subject of *Dasein*. In his seminar on *Heraclitus*, he claimed that the French translation of *Dasein* as "being-there" (*être-là*) had resulted in the loss of "everything that was gained as a new position in *Being and Time*" (see *Heraclitus Seminar, 1966–1967*, trans. Charles H. Seibert [University, Ala.: Alabama University Press, 1979], p. 126; with Eugene Fink). However, in a 1945 letter to Jean Beaufret, Heidegger makes clear that *Dasein* carried for him precisely the actional sense that I am about to impute to it. He writes that the word means "being-the-there." In so doing, he imputes to *Dasein* the status of being "the unconcealment of *aletheia*" (see Francoise Dastur, *Heidegger and the Question of Time*, trans. Francoise Raffoul and David Pettigrew [Atlantic Highlands, N.J.: Humanities Press International, 1998], p. 72.

5. Martin Heidegger, "Letter on Humanism," in *Basic Writings*, ed. David Farrell Krell (San Francisco: HarperSanFrancisco, 1993), p. 217.

6. Heidegger, *Being and Time*, p. 146.

7. Heidegger, *Being and Time*, p. 59. This would seem the moment to note once again that whereas concepts like "light," "visibility," and "invisibility" have for me a literal significance, they have for Heidegger a metaphoric meaning.

8. As Heidegger repeatedly stresses, this fallen or inauthentic *Dasein* is not something we can ever permanently transcend. It is a feature of every subjectivity. "Fallenness" is thus finally less a moral than a descriptive category.

9. "Presence-at-hand" is a feature of things in their ontic or preontological form. Human beings can never be present-at-hand, although we often mistakenly impute that status to them. See *Being and Time*, p. 150.

10. For a fuller discussion of the given-to-be-seen, a category which I take from Lacan, see my *The Threshold of the Visible World* (New York: Routledge, 1996), pp. 175–79.

11. Heidegger, *Being and Time*, p. 297.

12. For a general discussion of Being-towards-death, see *Being and Time*, pp. 304–11.

13. In *Being and Time*, p. 435, Heidegger writes "As thrown, [*Dasein*] has been submitted to a 'world,' and exists factically with others." He goes on in the same paragraph to associate the "factical" with *Dasein*'s "heritage."

14. Giorgio Agamben also suggests that our insertion into language constitutes a crucial feature of our "thrownness." In "Vocation and Voice" (trans. Jeff Fort; *Qui Parle* 10, no. 2 [1997]: 95) he writes: "Man . . . stands in the opening of being and of language without a voice, without a nature: he is thrown and abandoned in this opening, and from this abandon he must make his world, from language his own voice."

15. I take this phrase from Jacques Lacan, whose uses it in "Function and Field of Speech and Language in Psychoanalysis," in *Écrits: A Selection*, trans. Alan Sheridan (New York: Norton, 1977), p. 48.

16. Heidegger, *Being and Time*, p. 330.

17. The German word for guilt—*die Schuld*—means "debts" in its plural form, and "to owe" in its verbal form.

18. For Heidegger's discussion of guilt and the call to care, see *Being and Time*, pp. 312–48.

19. For Lacan's most extensive discussion of language, and the ways in which it precedes and exceeds us, see "The Function and Field of Speech and Language in Psychoanalysis," *Écrits*, pp. 30–113.

20. Heidegger offers a similar argument in ". . . Poetically Man Dwells . . . ," in *Poetry, Language, Thought*, trans. Albert Hofstadter (New York: Harper and Row, 1971), where he maintains that "language remains the master of man" (215), and where he insists that "strictly, it is language that speaks" (216). See also Heidegger, "Building Dwelling Thinking," in

Basic Writings, p. 348; and "The Way to Language," in *On the Way to Language*, trans. Peter D. Hertz (San Francisco: HarperSanFrancisco, 1982), pp. 111–36.

21. Lacan, "Function and Field of Speech and Language in Psychoanalysis," p. 104.

22. Lacan uses the metaphor of "fading" in *Four Fundamental Concepts of Psycho-Analysis*, trans. Alan Sheridan (New York: Norton, 1978), p. 208.

23. Lacan presents this account of the entry into language in *Four Fundamental Concepts of Psycho-Analysis*, pp. 203–29.

24. In *The Seminar of Jacques Lacan, Book VII: The Ethics of Psychoanalysis, 1959–1960*, trans. Dennis Porter (New York: Norton, 1992), p. 195, Lacan writes: "It is in the signifier and insofar as the subject articulates a signifying chain that he comes up against the fact that he may disappear from the chain of what is." Lacan himself uses the construction "being-for-death" (or in French, *être-pour-la-mort*) to refer to what Heidegger calls "Being-towards-death" (see "Function and Field of Speech and Language in Psychoanalysis," p. 68).

25. Jacques Lacan, *Four Fundamental Concepts of Psycho-Analysis*, trans. Alan Sheridan (New York: Norton, 1977), pp. 203–29.

26. I am drawing here upon the account of linguistic relations offered by Ferdinand de Saussure in *Course in General Linguistics*, trans. Wade Baskin (New York: McGraw-Hill, 1966).

27. Claude Lévi-Strauss, *The Elementary Structures of Kinship*, trans. James Harle Bell, John Richard von Sturmer, and Rodney Needham (Boston: Beacon, 1969), pp. 3–68.

28. For Lacan's discussion of *das Ding*, see *The Seminar of Jacques Lacan, Book VII*, pp. 43–154.

29. See Lacan, *The Seminar of Jacques Lacan, Book VII*, pp. 43–84, 101–14.

30. Jean-Joseph Goux, *Symbolic Economies: After Marx and Freud*, trans. Jennifer Curtiss Gage (Ithaca, N.Y.: Cornell University Press, 1990), p. 9.

31. As I will attempt to show in Chapter 6, the temporal relation between these two events is very complex. What ostensibly comes later can be said in at least one respect to precede what ostensibly comes earlier.

32. See, for instance, *The Seminar of Jacques Lacan, Book VII*, pp. 19–70; "The Signification of the Phallus," in *Écrits*, pp. 281–91; and the many discussions of the *Vorstellungsrepräsentanz* in *Four Fundamental*

Concepts of Psycho-Analysis. For a rather different clarification of this issue from the one I am offering here, see my "The Lacanian Phallus," *Differences* 4, no. 1 (1992): 84–115.

33. Sigmund Freud, "Mourning and Melancholia," in *The Standard Edition*, vol. 14, pp. 255–56.

34. Heidegger, "The Thing," *Poetry, Language, Thought*, pp. 172–74.

35. See Sigmund Freud, *The Interpretation of Dreams*, in *The Standard Edition*, vols. 4 and 5; *The Psychopathology of Everyday Life*, vol. 6; and *Jokes and Their Relation to the Unconscious*, vol. 8.

36. Sigmund Freud, "From the History of an Infantile Neurosis," in *The Standard Edition*, vol. 17, pp. 90–97.

37. Sigmund Freud, "Fetishism," in *The Standard Edition*, vol. 21, pp. 152–54.

38. This is my translation of the German text, which reads: "Der Tod ist der Schrein des Nichts, dessen nämlich, was in aller Hinsicht niemals etwas bloß Seiendes ist, was aber gleichwohl west, nämlich al das Sein Selbst." See Martin Heidegger, "Das Ding," in *Bremer und Freiburgere Vorträge*, in *Gesamtausgabe* (Frankfurt am Main: Vittorio Klostermann, 1949), p. 18.

39. The relevant pages of this section of *The Seminar of Jacques Lacan, Book VII* are 115–23.

40. As Marx helps us to understand in *Capital* (trans. Ben Fowkes [New York: Vintage, 1977], vol. 1, pp. 138–77), these are the two forms which exchange value can take. With the notion of relative value, Marx emphasizes the extrinsic nature of a commodity's value—the commodity's dependence upon another commodity for the manifestation of its worth. In the most primitive form of exchange, a commodity's relative value is determined by the other commodity which is exchanged for it. In a more "advanced," money form of exchange, a commodity's value is determined by the amount of money which is exchanged for it. Exchange value is the kind of value a commodity has when it has the function of representing the worth of another commodity.

41. Heidegger was hostile to all forms of thought predicated upon the notion of value. For his most extended critique of this notion, see *Nietzsche*, vols. 3 and 4.

42. See, for instance, Heidegger, "Letter on Humanism," in *Basic Writings*, ed. David Farrell Krell (San Francisco: HarperSanFrancisco, 1977), pp. 217–65.

43. The passage in question is Revelations 10.9–10.

44. "The Thing," p. 179. The German here reads *enteignende Vereignen* (see "Das Ding," p. 18).

CHAPTER 3: *Listening to Language*

1. I take this metaphor from Lacan, who uses it in "The Function and Field of Speech and Language in Psychoanalysis," in *Écrits: A Selection*, trans. Alan Sheridan (New York: Norton, 1977), p. 43.

2. Within the context of this book, the concepts of "possession" and "having" are in implicit opposition to those of "owning," "claiming," and "appropriating." Whereas owning, claiming and appropriating all entail the dissipation of the ego, it is at the behest of the ego that the subject attempts to possess or to have.

3. Martin Heidegger, *An Introduction to Metaphysics*, trans. Ralph Manheim (New Haven, Conn.: Yale University Press, 1959), p. 205.

4. Although Heidegger gives this concept increasing importance over time, it is already present in his earlier work. See, for instance, *Being and Time*, pp. 117, 396, 405; and "On the Essence of Truth" (1930), in *Basic Writings*, ed. David Farrell Krell (San Francisco: HarperSanFrancisco, 1993), pp. 124–32.

5. Martin Heidegger, "Letter on Humanism," *Basic Writings*, ed. David Farrell Krell, p. 217.

6. Martin Heidegger, "The Nature of Language," in *On the Way to Language*, trans. Peter D. Hertz (San Francisco: HarperSanFrancisco, 1971), p. 75.

7. Martin Heidegger, ". . . Poetically Man Dwells . . . ," in *Poetry, Language, Thought*, trans. Albert Hofstadter (New York: Harper and Row, 1971), p. 216.

8. Martin Heidegger, *Parmenides*, trans. André Schuwer and Rochard Rojcewicz (Bloomington: Indiana University Press, 1992), p. 12.

9. Martin Heidegger, "The Way to Language," in *On the Way to Language*, p. 128.

10. The German word which the translators of *On the Way to Language* render as "to appropriate" is *ereignen*. In common usage, this verb means "to take place or occur." The corresponding noun, *das Ereignis*, means "event." The occurrence which, more than any other, is for Heidegger deserving of the appellation *das Ereignis*, is of course disclosure. In his characteristic gesture of listening to language, Heidegger hears two other words contained within *ereignen*: *eignen*, which means "to suit or

be appropriate for," and *eigen*, meaning "one's own." These concepts become the basis for his conceptualization of the event of disclosure as an appropriation.

11. Jacques Lacan, "Function and Field of Speech and Language in Psychoanalysis," p. 104. This essay is also known as the Rome discourse.

12. Heidegger, "The Nature of Language," p. 62.

13. Martin Heidegger, "The Thing," in *Poetry, Language, Thought*, pp. 165–86.

14. Lacan himself says that a *word* is "a presence made of absence." However, as I will indicate in a moment, it is finally about things that he is speaking here.

15. Freud recounts the story of the *fort/da* game in *Beyond the Pleasure Principle*, in *The Standard Edition of the Complete Psychological Works*, trans. James Strachey (London: Hogarth, 1955), vol. 18, pp. 14–17.

16. Jacques Lacan, *The Seminar of Jacques Lacan, Book I: Freud's Papers on Technique, 1953–54*, trans. John Forrester (New York: Norton, 1991), pp. 242–43. Although Lacan imputes this idea to Hegel, he makes it central to his own argument. It is via the concept, he tells us, that the word confers time upon the thing.

17. See Jacques Lacan, *The Seminar of Jacques Lacan, Book VII: The Ethics of Psychoanalysis, 1959–60*, trans. Dennis Porter (New York: Norton, 1992), pp. 19–127.

18. For references to Saussure, see Jacques Lacan, "The Freudian Thing," in *Écrits*, p. 125; "The Agency of the Letter in the Unconscious," in *Écrits*, pp. 149, 154, and 160; and "Subversion of the Subject and the Dialectic of Desire," in *Écrits*, p. 298. For references to Lévi-Strauss, see "Function and Field of Speech and Language in Psychoanalysis," pp. 65–68. Lacan's theorizing of kinship structure as a language is massively indebted to Lévi-Strauss.

19. "Agency of the Letter in the Unconscious," p. 160.

20. Freud's *Project for a Scientific Psychology* can be found in *The Standard Edition*, vol. 1, pp. 295–387. For Lacan's discussion of this text, see *The Seminar of Jacques Lacan, Book VII*, pp. 19–84.

21. For a further definition of the *Bahnung*, see Chapter 4.

22. Martin Heidegger, "The Origin of the Work of Art," in *Poetry, Language, Thought*, p. 67.

23. Sigmund Freud, *Beyond the Pleasure Principle*, pp. 12–14.

24. Sigmund Freud, "The Uncanny," in *The Standard Edition*, vol. 17, p. 237.

25. Freud, *Beyond the Pleasure Principle*, p. 22.

26. Repetition in fact means a whole host of contradictory things in *Beyond the Pleasure Principle*. For a discussion of the many meanings this word sustains there, see my *Male Subjectivity at the Margins* (New York: Routledge, 1992), chap. 2.

27. Freud's discussion of binding is dispersed throughout the whole of *Beyond the Pleasure Principle*. For his analysis of linguistic repetition as a mastery of the past, see pp. 14–17. For his discussion of a therapeutic retelling of the past, see pp. 18–20.

28. Jacques Lacan, "The Freudian Thing," in *Écrits*, pp. 114–17.

29. I take this notion from Jean-Luc Godard's film, *Le Gai Savoir*.

30. Although these words come from *Being and Time*, they are quoted approvingly by Lacan in "Function and Field of Speech and Language in Psychoanalysis," p. 103. Sheridan gives p. 294 of the Macquarrie and Robinson translation as the source of this quote. Although the latter is close in spirit to the passage cited by Lacan, it does not match up at any point in a precise way with it.

31. Lacan, "Function and Field of Speech and Language in Psychoanalysis," p. 86.

32. Jacques Lacan, *The Seminar of Jacques Lacan, Book I*, pp. 109, 244.

33. For Freud's account of the transference, see "The Dynamics of Transference," in *The Standard Edition*, vol. 12, pp. 97–108; "Remembering, Repeating and Working-Through (Further Recommendations on the Technique of Psycho-Analysis II)," in *The Standard Edition*, vol. 12, pp. 145–56; and "Observations on Transference-Love (Further Recommendations on the Technique of Psycho-Analysis III)," in *The Standard Edition*, vol. 12, pp. 157–71.

34. In "Function and Field of Speech and Language in Psychoanalysis," Lacan writes: "For in its symbolizing function speech is moving towards nothing less than a transformation of the subject to whom it is addressed by means of the link that it establishes with the one who emits it—in other words, by introducing the effect of a signifier" (83).

35. Lacan attributes to the analyst the function of "punctuating" the analysand's discourse, most notably through the variable length of the analytic session ("Function and Field of Speech and Language in Psychoanalysis," p. 44).

36. This is how Saussure frames the distinction in *Course in General Linguistics*, pp. 87 and 98–100.

37. See especially pp. 123–27 of "The Way to Language."

38. Since both my musicological readers and those who will never forgive me for renouncing the negativity of *Male Subjectivity* are likely to cry foul at this point, I will take the liberty of pointing out that we refer to a certain very melancholy form of singing as "the blues," and that its aficionados can often be heard to say: "I love the blues."

39. I use the word "possession" here in a traditional sense. It therefore represents the antithesis of the concepts of "owning" and "claiming," which at least within the context of this book imply the negation rather than the triumph of the ego.

40. For the elaboration of a corresponding art history, see Mieke Bal, *Quoting Caravaggio: Contemporary Art, Preposterous History* (Chicago: University of Chicago Press, 1999).

CHAPTER 4: *Apparatus for the Production of an Image*

1. See Ferdinand de Saussure, *Course in General Linguistics*, trans. Wade Baskin (New York: McGraw-Hill, 1966), pp. 9 and 13–14.

2. *The Compact Oxford English Dictionary* (Oxford: Clarendon, 1991), p. 63.

3. This is how John Macquarrie and Edward Robinson render *Das Man* in their translation of *Sein and Zeit*. See *Being and Time* (San Francisco: HarperSanFrancisco, 1962). *Das Man* is Heidegger's name for what we are when we are not "ourselves." It is used in German in equivalent ways to "one" in English.

4. See, for instance, *The Interpretation of Dreams*, in *The Standard Edition of the Complete Psychological Works*, trans. James Strachey (London: Hogarth, 1953), vol. 5, p. 456.

5. This is one of the most fundamental tenets of Freudian thought, and a concept at the heart not only of *Interpretation of Dreams*, but also of Freud's *Jokes and Their Relation to the Unconscious* (*The Standard Edition*, vol. 8) and *The Psychopathology of Everyday Life* (vol. 6).

6. Joseph Breuer and Sigmund Freud, *Studies on Hysteria*, in *The Standard Edition*, vol. 2, pp. 59, 84. For a further discussion of the capacity of words to erase images, see the next chapter.

7. See Freud's discussion of Dora's two dreams in "Fragment of an Analysis of a Case of Hysteria," in *The Standard Edition*, vol. 7, pp. 64–111; his discussion of Hans's horse phobia in "Analysis of a Phobia in a Five-Year-Old Boy," in *The Standard Edition*, vol. 10, pp. 23–25; and his account of the Wolfman's dream and the primal scene in "From the History of an Infantile Neurosis," in *The Standard Edition*, vol. 17, pp. 29–47.

8. Sigmund Freud, *Beyond the Pleasure Principle*, in *The Standard Edition*, vol. 18, pp. 12–19.

9. The words *diegetic* and *extradiegetic*, which are extensively deployed within film studies, mean "interior to the fiction," and "exterior to the fiction."

10. This is Freud's own definition of negation, as offered in "Negation," in *The Standard Edition*, vol. 19, pp. 235–39.

11. For an excellent discussion of the navel of the dream, and one which remains closer to Freud's account of it than to my own, see Sam Weber, *The Legend of Freud* (Minneapolis: University of Minnesota Press, 1982), pp. 65–83.

12. For a very fine analysis of this logic of substitution, and of the sexual politics that subtends it, see Shoshana Felman, "Postal Survival, or the Question of the Navel," in *Yale French Studies*, no. 69 (1985): 49–72.

13. This is how Freud himself refers to the dream of Irma's injection in *Interpretation of Dreams, The Standard Edition*, vol. 4, pp. 107–21.

14. Freud discusses this dream in detail on two different occasions in *Interpretation of Dreams*. See *The Standard Edition*, vol. 4, pp. 169–76 and 281–84.

15. Although Strachey renders the entire transcript of the dream in the past tense, Freud himself renders it in the present up to this point. See *Die Traumdeutung*, in Sigmund Freud, *Studienausgabe*, ed. Alexander Mitscherlich, Angela Richards, and James Strachey (Frankfurt am Main: Fischer Verlag, 1972), vol. 2, pp. 436–37.

16. Sigmund Freud, "The Future of an Illusion," in *The Standard Edition*, vol. 21, p. 17.

17. Sigmund Freud, *Die Traumdeutung*, p. 512.

18. See Freud, *Interpretation of Dreams, The Standard Edition*, vol. 5, pp. 615–16; *Beyond the Pleasure Principle*, p. 25; and "A Note upon the 'Mystic Writing-Pad,'" in *The Standard Edition*, vol. 19, pp. 227–32.

19. The notion of a locality is only one of the metaphors through which Freud conceptualizes the preconscious and the unconscious in *Interpretation of Dreams*. He also conceptualizes them later as processes. See *The Standard Edition*, vol. 5, pp. 588–609, for this more dynamic account of the psyche.

20. Sigmund Freud, "The Unconscious," in *The Standard Edition*, vol. 14, p. 201.

21. Ibid.

22. Freud, *Beyond the Pleasure Principle*, p. 24.

23. *Interpretation of Dreams, The Standard Edition*, vol. 5, p. 541, fig. 3. Consciousness does not overtly figure within this diagram. Rather, the preconscious seems to represent the final destination of any given perception. However, "preconscious" here signifies not only the reserve of verbally organized memories, but the last stage before consciousness.

24. The German here is *Wahrnehmungsidentität* (*Die Traumdeutung*, p. 539).

25. Freud, *Interpretation of Dreams, The Standard Edition*, vol. 5, pp. 566–67.

26. Ibid., p. 616.

27. Freud, "Repression," in *The Standard Edition*, vol. 14, p. 148.

28. Freud, *Die Traumdeutung*, p. 522.

29. Sigmund Freud, *Project for a Scientific Psychology*, in *The Standard Edition*, vol. 1, p. 361.

30. Although, on p. 8 of *Beyond the Pleasure Principle*, Freud correlates the degree of pleasure experienced by the subject to the degree of diminution in the state of excitation, making complete evacuation the epitome of pleasure, on p. 9 he suggests that the pleasure principle may also be a constancy principle. As Jean Laplanche argues in *Life and Death in Psychoanalysis* (trans. Jeffrey Mehlman [Baltimore: Johns Hopkins University Press, 1976], pp. 103–24), the two definitions are incompatible with each other.

31. Freud, *Interpretation of Dreams, The Standard Edition*, vol. 5, p. 538. The German here reads *Reflexapparat*.

32. Ibid., pp. 565–67.

33. Ibid., p. 616.

34. The distinction between fore-pleasure and end-pleasure is one Freud makes in *Three Essays on a Theory of Sexuality*, in *The Standard Edition*, vol. 7, p. 210.

35. The notion that excitatory quantity can be commuted into affective quality is one which Freud himself broaches in *Project for a Scientific Psychology*, pp. 309 and 312.

36. Lacan provides a similar definition of the pleasure principle in *The Seminar of Jacques Lacan, Book VII: The Ethics of Psychoanalysis, 1959–1960*, trans. Dennis Porter (New York: Norton, 1992). On p. 58, he writes: "The pleasure principle governs the search for the object and imposes the detours which maintain the distance in relation to its end. . . . The transfer-

ence of the quantity from *Vorstellung* to *Vorstellung* always maintains the search at a certain distance from that which it gravitates around." See also pp. 51 and 57.

37. See, for instance, "Das Unbewuste," in *Studienausgabe*, vol. 3, p. 159.

38. Martin Heidegger, "The Age of the World Picture," in *A Question Concerning Technology and Other Essays*, trans. William Lovitt (New York: Harper and Row, 1977), p. 129.

39. Mikkel Borch-Jacobsen, *The Freudian Subject*, trans. Catherine Porter (Stanford, Calif.: Stanford University Press, 1988), pp. 4–5.

40. Ibid., pp. 1–52.

41. As I will indicate in a moment, Freud himself acknowledges that it is often ourselves whom we most seek to see.

42. I take the notion of "belong-to-me-ness" from Lacan. In *Four Fundamental Concepts of Psycho-Analysis* (trans. Alan Sheridan [New York: Norton, 1978], p. 81), he writes, in tacit reference to Heidegger: "The privilege of the subject seems to be established here from that bipolar reflexive relation by which, as soon as I perceive, my representations belong to me."

43. See also Freud, *Interpretation of Dreams, The Standard Edition*, vol. 4, 322–23; and vol. 5, 440–41.

44. The text from which Freud here quotes is Karl Albert Scherner, *Das Leben des Traumes* (Berlin: Verlag con Heinrich Shindler, 1861).

45. In *Seminar VII*, Lacan suggests that the ego is a mirage concealing the subject's *manque-à-être* (298).

46. Freud, *Interpretation of Dreams*, in *The Standard Edition*, vol. 5, p. 544.

47. *The Compact Oxford English Dictionary*, p. 1542.

48. For the passage to which I refer, see Martin Heidegger, *Parmenides*, trans. André Schuwer and Richard Rojcewicz (Bloomington: Indiana University Press, 1992), p. 107. Although in this passage the look once again provides Heidegger with a metaphor for talking about disclosure, it comes close at moments to subordinating what it ostensibly represents.

49. Although this is a crucial Heideggerian concept, it does not appear in the passage in *Parmenides* devoted to the look. I am here reading this passage together with *Being and Time*.

CHAPTER 5: *The Milky Way*

1. Sigmund Freud, "The Unconscious," appendix C, *Standard Edition of the Complete Psychological Works*, trans. James Strachey (London: Hogarth, 1957), vol. 14, pp. 213–14. There are some terminological discrepan-

cies between this monograph and *The Interpretation of Dreams* in the language the two use to refer to word-presentations and thing-presentations. "The Unconscious" can also be found in vol. 14 of *The Standard Edition*, pp. 166–208.

2. Joseph Breuer and Sigmund Freud, *Studies on Hysteria*, in *The Standard Edition*, vol. 2, p. 7.

3. See *Studies on Hysteria*, pp. 24–40, for Breuer's account of Anna O.'s "absences."

4. Freud, "The Unconscious," appendix C, pp. 213–14.

5. Ferdinand de Saussure, *Course in General Linguistics*, trans. Wade Baskin (New York: McGraw Hill, 1966), p. 103.

6. Freud, *The Interpretation of Dreams*, *The Standard Edition*, vol. 5, pp. 566–67 and 602.

7. See Freud, *Interpretation of Dreams*, *The Standard Edition*, vol. 5, pp. 602–3 and 617; and "The Unconscious," *The Standard Edition*, vol. 14, pp. 201–3.

8. Freud, *Interpretation of Dreams*, *The Standard Edition*, vol. 5, p. 574.

9. For Freud's primary discussions of binding, see *Project for a Scientific Psychology*, in *The Standard Edition*, vol. 1, pp. 380–81; and *Beyond the Pleasure Principle*, in *The Standard Edition*, vol. 18, pp. 7–64. Freud associates binding with the linguistic organization of our memories on pp. 12–17 of the second of these two books.

10. See Freud, *Interpretation of Dreams*, *The Standard Edition*, vol. 5, pp. 610–11.

11. See Freud, *Project for a Scientific Psychology*, pp. 323 and 368; *Interpretation of Dreams*, *The Standard Edition*, vol. 5, p. 599; and "The Unconscious," p. 188.

12. For a discussion of this notion of equal investment, which Freud will later associate more with the ego than with the preconscious, see Jean Laplanche, *Life and Death in Psychoanalysis*, trans. Jeffrey Mehlman (Baltimore: Johns Hopkins University Press, 1976), pp. 62–65.

13. In the diagrams with which Freud accounts for the perceptual event in *Interpretation of Dreams*, perceptual stimuli arrive at consciousness only after passing through both the unconscious and the preconscious, and hence being worked over psychically in all kinds of ways (see *The Standard Edition*, vol. 5, pp. 537–41).

14. Freud, "The Unconscious," p. 202.

15. This discussion of language as the negation of the perceptual signifier was inspired by some remarks made by Lacan in *The Seminar of*

Jacques Lacan, Book VII, trans. Dennis Porter (New York: Norton, 1992), pp. 64–65.

16. Freud, "The Unconscious," p. 186.

17. Freud, "Negation," in *The Standard Edition*, vol. 19, p. 236.

18. Ibid., pp. 235–36.

19. Freud, "The Unconscious," appendix C, pp. 213–14.

20. Freud, "The Unconscious," p. 190.

21. Freud, *Aus den Anfängen der Psychoanalyse*, ed. Marie Bonaparte, Anna Freud, and Ernst Kris (London: Imago, 1950), pp. 309–11; *Project for a Scientific Psychology*, pp. 300–302.

22. Although Freud does not himself characterize this pathway as the *Bahnung*, his account of it suggests that he saw it as the preferred pathway for the flow of Anna O.'s psychic energy during the period of her illness. Interestingly, he accounts for the talking cure as the reorganization of Anna O.'s memories into tidy dossiers (288–89).

23. Freud, "Instincts and Their Vicissitudes," in *The Standard Edition*, vol. 14, p. 122.

24. Freud remarks in "Repression," in *The Standard Edition*, vol. 14, that the drive energy which is attached to a particular memory can be affected by repression in one of three ways: it can be changed into anxiety, manifest itself in the guise of another affect, or it can be suppressed (153). However, regardless of which of these alternatives is deployed, it is the nature of this force to "return" in the guise of subsitutory formations (154).

25. Ibid., p. 148.

26. In his translation of "The Unconscious," Strachey writes: "protecting rampart" (183). The German, however, reads *schützende Wall*. See Sigmund Freud, "Das Unbewußte," in *Freud- Studienausgabe*, ed. Alexander Mitscherlich, Angela Richards, and James Strachey (Frankfurt am Main: S. Fischer, 1969–75), vol. 3, p. 142.

27. Although Freud represents anticathexis as a normal part of repression, he illustrates it with an example drawn from a phobia (184). I am at a loss to account for this negative characterization.

28. The metapsychological papers include "Instincts and Their Vicissitudes," "Repression," and "The Unconscious."

29. I draw in part here upon Lacan's account of repression in *Seminar VII*, pp. 43–70.

30. Lacan usually privileges the linguistic over the perceptual signifier when describing how the subject enters language. In both "Function and Field of Speech and Language in Psychoanalysis" (in *Écrits: A Selection*,

trans. Alan Sheridan [Norton: New York, 1977], pp. 103–4) and in *Four Fundamental Concepts of Psycho-Analysis* (trans. Alan Sheridan [New York: Norton, 1978], p. 239), for instance, Lacan uses the *fort/da* story Freud tells in *Beyond the Pleasure Principle* to dramatize what it means to speak for the first time. Through the articulation of two paradigmatically opposed phonemes, which stand for something like "gone" and "here," the infant subject enters a closed order of signification which alienates it from "presence" or the "here and now." In the somewhat different version of this foundational narrative which Lacan recounts in "The Signification of the Phallus," in *Écrits*, pp. 281–91, the emphasis falls more upon the symbolization of loss than its production. It is, we learn, via the image of the penis that we acquire the metaphoric wherewithal to understand what we have lost. Nevertheless, this little scenario of vision remains subordinate to and referential of the linguistic drama which precedes it.

In *Seminar VII*, however, Lacan refuses to privilege the linguistic signifier in this way. He suggests at one point that since word-presentations are always linked to thing-presentations, no hard and fast distinction can be made between them (45). The only indispensable precondition for the entry into language is the positioning of one term in the place of another. Most of the time, moreover, he attributes to the perceptual signifier both a more originary and a more important central psychic role than the linguistic signifier (see, for instance, pp. 65, 138). Words by themselves, he tells us at one point, could never get us inside signification. It is, rather, by means of the predominantly visual thing-presentation that we begin to speak (65).

31. See *Beyond the Pleasure Principle*, p. 30, and "The Unconscious," pp. 183 and 193.

32. I take this metaphor from Lacan, who uses it in *Four Fundamental Concepts of Psycho-Analysis*, p. 208.

33. For Lacan's association of dignity with *das Ding*, see *Seminar VII*, p. 112.

34. *Vorstellung* is the German word for "representation." *Vorstellungsrepräsentanz* is Freud's term for "ideational representative."

35. Freud, *Beyond the Pleasure Principle*, pp. 55–56.

36. Lacan emphasizes the nonrepresentative status of the first representative of "being" in *Four Fundamental Concepts of Psycho-Analysis*, pp. 217–18.

37. This is the primary reason why Lacan's account of the relation between primal and secondary repression in "The Signification of the

Phallus" is finally so unbelievable. He attempts to predicate the signifying relation between "being" and "phallus" on the basis of the properties of the latter (287). Of course, knowing full well that this is an untenable proposition, Lacan prefaces his enumeration of the similarities between "being" and "phallus" with the words "it could be said." However, as Jane Gallop points out in *Reading Lacan* (Ithaca, N.Y.: Cornell University Press, 1985), pp. 154–56, these words permit him to assert the representational relation of phallus to "being" while ostensibly denying it.

38. I say "hypothetically" because there are clearly cultural forces working to determine which ideational representative is chosen.

39. Lacan also insists upon the nonmeaning of the first term that takes the place of "being" in *Four Fundamental Concepts of Psycho-Analysis*, p. 211.

40. Freud tells the *fort/da* story, which almost always figures in Lacan's account of the entry into language, in *Beyond the Pleasure Principle*, pp. 14–17.

41. See Lacan, "On a Question Preliminary to Any Possible Treatment of Psychosis," in *Écrits*, pp. 179–225; and *The Seminar of Jacques Lacan, Book III: The Psychoses, 1955–56*, trans. Russell Grigg (New York: Norton, 1993).

42. Lacan provides a particular precise formulation of the relation between the mother and *das Ding* on p. 67.

43. See Lacan, "Desire and the Interpretation of Desire in *Hamlet*," trans. James Hulbert, *Yale French Studies*, nos. 55 and 56 (1977): 11–52.

44. Freud, "The Unconscious," p. 190.

45. Lacan, *The Seminar of Jacques Lacan, Book VII*, p. 45.

46. So far as I have been able to ascertain, this is Lacan's word, not Freud's. See *The Seminar of Jacques Lacan: Book VII*, p. 49.

47. Sigmund Freud, "A Metapsychological Supplement to the Theory of Dreams," in *The Standard Edition*, vol. 14, p. 231.

48. Marcel Proust is for me the writer whose language is most visual. For a brilliant discussion of this feature of his writing, see Mieke Bal, *The Mottled Screen: Reading Proust Visually*, trans. Anna-Louise Milne (Stanford, Calif.: Stanford University Press, 1997).

49. I refer here to Freud's dream of the botanical monograph, recounted on pp. 169–76 and 282–84 of *The Interpretation of Dreams*, in *The Standard Edition*, vol. 4. I discuss both this dream and the dream of Irma's injection in Chapter 4.

50. For Freud's analysis of the dream of Irma's injection, see *Interpretation of Dreams*, *The Standard Edition*, vol. 4, pp. 106–18.

CHAPTER 6: *The Language of Things*

1. Genesis 2.19. We are not told here that Adam named the things of paradise, only the creatures. However, I am reading the latter as a synecdoche for everything God is supposed to have created.

2. For Descartes's proof of his own existence through reference to his thought, see *Discourse on Method*, in *Discourse on Method and Meditations on First Philosophy*, ed. David Weissman (New Haven, Conn.: Yale University Press, 1996), pp. 21–22.

3. The phrase "supersensible substrate" derives from Immanuel Kant, who uses it to describe the concept on the basis of which aesthetic judgment comes into play. See *Critique of Judgement*, trans. J. H. Bernard (New York: Hafner, 1951), p. 185.

4. Perceptual identity occurs when there is a coalescence of memory and perceptual stimuli. It is the end toward which all mental activities are directed. See Sigmund Freud, *Interpretation of Dreams*, in *The Standard Edition of the Complete Psychological Works*, trans. James Strachey (London: Hogarth, 1953), vol. 5, pp. 566–67 and 602.

5. In *Early Greek Thinking: The Dawn of Western Philosophy* (trans. David Farrell Krell and Frank A. Capuzzi [San Francisco: HarperSan Francisco, 1975], p. 56), Heidegger claims that "appearance is an essential consequence of presencing." Earlier in the same book, he writes that it is through the "presencing of what is present" that Being is disclosed (39). As I have argued earlier in this book, "presencing" is a psychic activity whose effect is temporalizing. It thus has nothing to do with the "here and now."

6. As will become clear, "intention" here signifies not conscious resolve, but an a-subjective "tending-toward."

7. Hannah Arendt, *The Life of the Mind* (New York: Harcourt, Brace, 1978), p. 19.

8. See Maurice Merleau-Ponty, *The Visible and the Invisible*, trans. Alphonso Lingis (Evanston, Ill.: Northwestern University Press, 1968), pp. 130–55; and Jacques Lacan, *Four Fundamental Concepts of Psycho-Analysis*, trans. Alan Sheridan (New York: Norton, 1978), pp. 67–119. For a reading of Lacan's account of the field of vision, see my *Male Subjectivity at the Margins* (New York: Routledge, 1992), pp. 125–56; and *The Threshold of the Visible World* (New York: Routledge, 1996), pp. 125–227.

9. Adolf Portmann, *Animal Forms and Patterns: A Study of the Appearance of Animals*, trans. Hella Czech (New York: Schocken, 1967), pp. 86, 201, and 294.

10. See Roger Caillois, "Mimicry and Legendary Psychasthenia," trans. John Shepley, *October*, no. 31 (Winter 1984): 17–32; *The Mask of Medusa*, trans. George Ordish (New York: Clarkson N. Potter, 1964); and *The Writing of Stones*, trans. Barbara Bray (Charlottesville: University Press of Virginia, 1985).

11. Caillois, *The Mask of Medusa*, p. 40.

12. Caillois, *The Writing of Stones*, pp. 37–43.

13. Caillois, "Mimicry and Legendary Psychasthenia," p. 23.

14. Caillois, *The Mask of Medusa*, p. 75.

15. Jacques Lacan, *Four Fundamental Concepts*, pp. 93–108.

16. Lacan himself distinguishes between *le regard* and *l'oeil* (see *Le Séminaire de Jacques Lacan, Livre XI: Les Quatre Concepts fondamentaux de la psychoanalyse* [Paris: Editions du Seuil, 1973], pp. 65–109), a distinction which Sheridan renders via "gaze" and "look."

17. Lacan, *Four Fundamental Concepts*, p. 107; *The Seminar of Jacques Lacan, Book I: Freud's Papers on Technique, 1953–1954*, trans. John Forrester (New York: Norton, 1988), p. 137.

18. Lacan, *Four Fundamental Concepts*, p. 107.

19. Jacques Lacan, *The Seminar of Jacques Lacan, Book II: The Ego in Freud's Theory and in the Technique of Psychoanalysis, 1954–1955*, trans. Sylvana Tomaselli (New York: Norton, 1991), p. 223.

20. I have been unable to locate this phrase in Portmann, but it is attributed to him by Arendt on p. 46 of *The Life of the Mind.*

21. Martin Heidegger, "The Way to Language," in *On the Way to Language*, trans. Peter D. Hertz (San Francisco: HarperSanFrancisco, 1971), p. 123.

22. Lacan, *Four Fundamental Concepts*, p. 76.

23. Maurice Merleau-Ponty, "Eye and Mind," in *The Merleau-Ponty Aesthetics Reader: Philosophy and Painting*, ed. Galen A. Johnson (Evanston, Ill.: Northwestern University Press, 1993), p. 141.

24. Maurice Merleau-Ponty, *Phenomenology of Perception*, trans. Colin Smith (London: Routledge and Kegan Paul, 1962), p. 320.

25. Martin Heidegger, *Parmenides*, trans. André Schuwer and Richard Rojcewicz (Bloomington: Indiana University Press, 1992), p. 107.

26. As Jean-Luc Nancy puts it in *The Sense of the World* (trans. Jeffrey S. Librett [Minneapolis: University of Minnesota Press, 1997], p. 61), Heidegger "fails to weigh precisely the weight of the stone that rolls or surges forth onto the earth, the weight of the *contact* of the stone with the other

surface, and through it with the world as the network of all surfaces. He misses the surface in general."

27. Merleau-Ponty, *Phenomenology of Perception*, p. 214.

28. The French text here reads: " *un extraordinaire concours de signes*" (Caillois's emphasis; see *L'Écriture des Pierres*, ed. Albert Skira [Geneva: Editions d'Art, 1970], p. 114), which the English translator renders "an extraordinary combination of signs."

29. Maurice Merleau-Ponty, "Indirect Language and the Voices of Silence," in *The Merleau-Ponty Aesthetics Reader: Philosophy and Painting*, p. 91.

30. Merleau-Ponty, *Phenomenology of Perception*, pp. 319.

31. Ibid., p. 316.

32. See Leo Bersani, *The Culture of Redemption* (Cambridge: Harvard University Press, 1990), and *Homos* (Cambridge: Harvard University Press, 1995); and Leo Bersani and Ulysse Dutoit, *The Forms of Violence: Narrative in Assyrian Art and Modern Culture* (New York: Schocken, 1985); *Arts of Impoverishment: Beckett, Rothko, Resnais* (Cambridge: Harvard University Press, 1993); and *Caravaggio's Secrets* (Cambridge: MIT Press, 1998).

33. In *The Culture of Redemption*, Bersani writes: "Phenomena do not 'mean' the other phenomena with which they enter into relation; it is as if each term of an analogy, for example, positioned itself more satisfactorily in the universe—completed itself—by thus contributing to the universe's always shifting designs" (75).

34. In *Arts of Impoverishment*, Bersani and Dutoit stress the second kind of communication of forms (see especially p. 6). In general, though, Bersani is more concerned with the first.

35. Bersani, *The Culture of Redemption*, p. 19; Bersani and Dutoit, *Arts of Impoverishment*, pp. 153–55.

36. I am quoting here very much out of context.

37. See "A Conversation with Leo Bersani," *October*, no. 82 (1997): 6.

38. It appears that this is not an actual quotation, but rather a sentence attributed to Cézanne by Merleau-Ponty on the basis of his reading of Cézanne's art.

39. Lacan refers at one point in *Four Fundamental Concepts* to paintings that induce the spectator to lay down the gaze. Significantly, he invokes in this context Merleau-Ponty's essay on Cézanne (pp. 109–10).

40. I take the notion of the "fading" of "being" from Lacan. See *Four Fundamental Concepts*, pp. 207–13. Lacan, however, here attributes this event to the linguistic rather than the perceptual signifier.

41. Merleau-Ponty, *The Visible and the Invisible,* p. 136.
42. In *The Structure of Behavior* (trans. Alden L. Fisher [Boston: Beacon, 1963], p. 186), Merleau-Ponty maintains that perspective is perhaps the "essential property" of things, and that it is because of this that "the perceived possesses in itself a hidden and inexhaustible richness."

INDEX

Agamben, Giorgio, 157n14
Allen, R. E., 150n22, 151n25
Annas, Julia, 149n18
appearance, 2–3, 43, 75, 136, 143–45; and art, 72–74; as collaboration of look and world, 20–21, 128–29. *See also* Being; desire; language of desire
appropriation (*Ereignis*), 54–55, 57, 69, 74, 145, 160n10
Arendt, Hannah, 24, 148n8–9, 149n14; on appearance, 2–3, 129–30, 155n62
art, 73–74, 132

Bahnung, die (facilitation), 58, 110–12, 119–120, 168n22
Bal, Mieke, 163n40, 170n48
Bartsch, Shadi, 151n24
beauty, 20–21, 25–26; and desire, 17, 92, 98, 133, 143, 145–46; in Plato, 8–10, 11, 128
Being: as appearance, 7, 19, 30, 132, 135–36; as becoming, 26–27; in Heidegger, 3, 7, 42, 53, 138; as more than reality, 16–17, 25–28, 144–45; in Plato, 17–18; as product of desire, 43, 46, 49–50, 59. *See also* appearance; desire; language of desire

Being-in-the-world, 28, 29, 34
Being-towards-death, 28, 33–34, 36, 45, 62, 65, 67
Benjamin, Walter, 10
Bersani, Leo, 141–42, 173n33
Borch-Jacobsen, Mikkel, 94–95
Butler, Judith, 154n49

Caillois, Roger, 131–36, 139, 173n28
care, 28, 32, 35, 47, 73, 100, 165n55; and appropriation, 55; and language of desire, 52, 60, 62, 144; and the Oedipus complex, 38–39
Cézanne, Paul, 58–59, 143–44, 173n38
clearing, the, 30, 46, 53–54, 56, 73, 79
Cobb, William S., 151n25
creation, 48–49, 56, 59, 92; in the Bible, 19–22, 128, 171n1; in Irigaray, 13–15; in Lacan, 15–17; in Plato, 11–15

Dasein, 23, 31–35, 44–45, 57, 156n4, 157n13; and kinship, 38; and time, 25. *See also* appropriation; Being-towards-death; care; language; temporality
Descartes, René, 31, 94–95, 128
desire, 11, 39–40, 78, 133, 144; and eating the book, 46–48; and

Cultural Memory | in the Present